TIME TO LISTEN

Hearing People on the Receiving End of International Aid

Mary B. Anderson
Dayna Brown
Isabella Jean

CDA Collaborative Learning Projects

Cambridge, Massachusetts

CDA Collaborative Learning Projects

17 Dunster Street, Suite 202

Cambridge, MA 02138

+1-617-661-6310

www.cda-collaborative.org

First Edition

© November 2012

ISBN: 978-0-9882544-1-1

Cover Images photographed by:

Isabella Jean

Björn Holmberg

Diego Devesa Laux

Layout and cover design by Ambit Creative Group

www.ambitcreativegroup.com

TABLE OF CONTENTS

Chapters

Appendices

PREFACE AND ACKNOWLEDGEMENTS

Preface

This book captures the experiences and voices of over 6,000 people who have received international assistance, observed the effects of aid efforts, or been involved in providing aid. Over time, across very different contexts and continents, people's experiences with international aid efforts have been remarkably consistent. While there was a wide range of opinions on specifics, the authors were struck by the similarity in people's descriptions of their interactions with the international aid system. Their stories are powerful and full of lessons for those who care enough to listen and to hear the ways that people on the receiving side of aid suggest it can become more effective and accountable.

We have not named people, agencies, or projects in this book. The authors have done this both to honor the privacy of conversations and to reflect the fact that any comment we quote represents a widely-shared viewpoint rather than that of a single individual. The Listening Project (through which these conversations occurred) was not evaluating individual projects or agencies, but instead focused on understanding the long-term, cumulative effects of different types of international aid efforts on people, communities, and their societies over time.

Some of the conversations reported in this book occurred as much as six years ago. The Listening Project was established in late 2005, and since then, a number of donors and aid agencies have adopted policies intended to address many of the issues raised by aid recipients. There is indeed a growing awareness that significant changes are needed to improve the effectiveness and accountability of international assistance. The Busan Partnership for Effective Development Co-operation and the New Deal for Engagement in Fragile States, agreed to by development actors from donor and recipient countries in late 2011, are some examples. However, in recent field visits and Feedback Workshops, we continue to hear exactly the same comments and analyses heard six years ago from people on the receiving end of aid efforts.

The conversations captured here show that the problems are not yet solved. The cumulative voice of people who live in aid-recipient societies provides a powerful—indeed a compelling—case for more radical and systemic change in the aid system. The authors can claim this because we do not "own" this book. Instead it is the product of the over 6,000 people who were willing to tell their stories and reflect on the patterns they had observed in how aid benefits, or fails to benefit, their societies. It is the product of the many other people whom we acknowledge here.

Acknowledgements

First and foremost, this book would not be possible without the commitment of time and insights from the many people to whom we listened in Aceh (Indonesia), Afghanistan, Angola, Bolivia, Bosnia-Herzegovina, Cambodia, Ecuador, Ethiopia, Kenya, Kosovo, Lebanon, Mali, Mindanao (Philippines), Myanmar/Burma, Solomon Islands, Sri Lanka, Thai-Burma border, Thailand, Timor-Leste, US Gulf Coast, and Zimbabwe. Their willingness to talk with Listening Teams about their experiences and perspectives has been inspiring and we are truly thankful for the time they gave to the Listening Project.

The many people who helped gather and analyze the evidence summarized in this book include the more than 400 Listening Team members who listened seriously and took notes during the conversations with people in recipient countries; the facilitators who enabled collaborative analysis and collated these notes; and finally the team leaders and writers who wrote each of the field visit reports (listed in Appendix 1).

The Listening Teams were made up of staff from international aid agencies and local organizations, with facilitators from CDA. Over 125 organizations participated in the 20 Listening Exercises which were hosted by different collaborating agencies in each country. Representatives from more than 150 donors, governments, aid agencies, local organizations, universities and others contributed their time in 16 Feedback Workshops and 2 consultations. Some organizations participated in numerous Listening Exercises and Feedback Workshops, while others just joined for one, but all were equally committed (all are listed in Appendix 2). This book would not be possible without their active engagement and significant contributions to this collaborative listening and learning effort.

Each Listening Exercise was led by various international and local facilitators, including a CDA staff member and/or external consultants. We would like to acknowledge and thank them for their valuable contribution to the Listening Project: Rames Abhukara (Mali); Dost Bardouille-Crema (Philippines); Diana Chigas (Bolivia); Antonio Donini (Afghanistan); Emily Farr (Zimbabwe); Winifred Fitzgerald (Mali); Susan Granada (Philippines); Natiq Hamidullah (Afghanistan); Greg Hansen (Lebanon); Björn Holmberg (Afghanistan); Paul Jeffery (Kosovo); Riva Kantowitz (Kosovo); Chuck Kleymeyer (Bolivia, Ecuador); Idrissa Maiga (Mali); Channsitha Mark (Myanmar/Burma); Veronika Martin (Angola, Cambodia, Lebanon, Sri Lanka, Thai-Burma Border); Jonathan Moore (Cambodia);

Dilshan Muhajarine (Sri Lanka); Vaso Neofotistos (Bosnia-Herzegovina); Smruti Patel (Thailand); Saji Prelis (Sri Lanka); Christopher Ramezanpour (Philippines); David Reyes (Angola, Kenya); Patricia Ringers (Thailand); Terry Rogocki (Sri Lanka); Kate Roll (Timor-Leste); Jonathan Rudy (Philippines); Frederica Sawyer (Ethiopia); Daniel Selener (Bolivia); Jim Shyne (Angola); Soth Plai Ngarm (Myanmar/Burma); Sibylle Stamm (Lebanon); Jean Tafoa (Solomon Islands); Nina Tuhaika (Solomon Islands); Leslie Tuttle (Zimbabwe); Marshall Wallace (Indonesia, Afghanistan); Andrew Wei-Chih Yang (Kosovo, Timor-Leste); Iris Wielders (Solomon Islands); Sue Williams (Myanmar/Burma); Peter Woodrow (Indonesia); and Luis Ximenes (Timor-Leste).

The Listening Project would not have been possible without the generous financial support of the Australian Agency for International Development (AusAID), Canadian International Development Agency (CIDA), UK Department for International Development (DFID), Swiss Agency for Development Cooperation (DEZA), German Federal Ministry for Economic Cooperation and Development (BMZ), Swedish International Development Cooperation Agency (SIDA), International Rescue Committee, International Federation of the Red Cross and Red Crescent Societies (IFRC), Catholic Relief Services, Mercy Corps, and Oxfam America. The participating agencies and hosts of Listening Exercises and Feedback Workshops also made significant in-kind contributions by providing information and coordination, staff time, vehicles, space, and other logistical support. Additionally, several networks and organizations invited and paid for Listening Project staff to make presentations and lead workshops on the methodology and field-based evidence.

Our CDA colleagues have cheerfully provided essential support throughout the listening process and helpful critiques of field visit reports, issue papers, policy briefs (listed in Appendix 3) and this book. We are particularly indebted to Steve Darvill who frequently joined the authors as we pondered the learning produced by this effort, to Andrew Yang who helped organize and coordinate Listening Exercises, Feedback Workshops, and Consultations, and to Candice Montalvo who led the entire publishing process and was a huge help in the writing of this book. We also thank our interns, Jessica Heinzelman and Elspeth Suthers, who helped with the coding of the field visit reports.

Lastly, we want to thank our families who supported our absences and excitement throughout the last six years of listening and learning.

Mary B. Anderson
Founder and former Executive Director of CDA Collaborative Learning Projects

Dayna Brown
Director, Listening Program

Isabella Jean
Director, Evaluation and Learning

CHAPTER ONE

INTRODUCTION

The Issue

Does the way that international assistance is now organized make sense? Is it reasonable for people in countries that have resources and know-how to provide these to people in countries that are deemed to need them? Is it reasonable to expect that doing so can contribute to overcoming poverty, alleviating suffering, supporting good governance, or mitigating conflict in the receiving societies? Is international assistance—as it is now delivered—working as we mean it to?

This book approaches these questions through the experiences of people on the receiving side of international assistance; it reports on the ideas, insights, and analyses of almost 6,000 people who live in countries where aid has been provided. These people, who have either directly received assistance or observed others in their societies doing so—sometimes in many forms and over many years—are the front-row observers of its processes and impacts. They see how the designs and intentions of the givers play out in people's lives and in social and political structures, cumulatively and over time.

From late 2005 through 2009, CDA Collaborative Learning Projects carried out a broad, systematic effort to listen to the voices of people who live in countries where international assistance has been given. More than 125 international and local aid organizations joined the Listening Project in 20 aid-recipient countries to talk with people about their experiences with, and judgments of, international assistance. The Listening Project held conversations with people who represented broad cross-sections of their societies, ranging from fishermen on the beach to government ministers with experience in bilateral aid negotiations. Local leaders and average villagers, government officials and civil society activists, teachers and students, small business owners and wealthy ones, men and women, young and old, dominant and marginalized groups were all included.

From such a range of locations and people, one might expect many ideas and opinions, and, indeed, the Listening Project heard a lot. However, cumulatively, from all these conversations with all these people in all these places, remarkably consistent patterns and common judgments emerged. In the midst of difference, there was striking unanimity and consistency about the processes and the effects of the international aid system.

A Brief Preview of What People Say

Universally, when asked to comment on their assessment of international assistance and its cumulative effects on their societies, people respond with, "International aid is a good thing, and we are grateful for it … but …." They cite a specific positive experience or two and express their appreciation for the people who care enough to help. However, after this, a "but" always follows. And then they begin an often thoughtful and clarifying analysis of how aid has worked and has not worked, and of how they believe it should and could work to make a more positive difference in their lives.

Many people talk about what they expected or hoped aid would do, and most say they were disappointed. Was this because their expectations were unrealistic, or was it because international assistance failed? Most say that both factors are present. They acknowledge that they expect too much, and they also say that, in their experience, the very processes and systems of the international aid system undermine its intended effectiveness.

Many describe how assistance begins as a boost to people's spirits and energies, but over time, becomes entrenched as an increasingly complicated system of reciprocated dependence. A number say that they believe aid providers depend on the recipients' "needs" because responding to these needs justifies the providers' existence and work. They also recognize that their countries, communities, and neighbors (and sometimes they, themselves) rely on continuing international assistance to function, even when this assistance creates a dependency that they dislike and decry.

Even as most aid providers focus on raising and allocating more funds to the assistance enterprise, people on the recipient side talk about using the funds already allocated in better ways. Very few people call for more aid; virtually everyone says they want "smarter" aid. Many feel that "too much" is given "too fast." A majority criticize the "waste" of money and other resources through programs they perceive as misguided or through the failure of aid providers to be sufficiently engaged.

The voices reported here convey four basic messages: first, international aid is a good thing that is appreciated; second, assistance as it is now provided is not achieving its intent; third, fundamental changes must be made in how aid is provided if it is to become an effective tool in support of positive economic, social, and political change; and fourth, these fundamental changes are both possible and doable.

What this Book Is Not; Who this Book Is Not Intended for

This book is *not*, however, another in the long (and growing) line of damning commentaries about the negative impacts of international assistance. Without doubt, international efforts to be helpful often fall short of their intentions to improve the conditions of life for people in recipient communities. Also without doubt, these efforts sometimes leave people worse off, rather than better off. To conclude, however, that aid is therefore a failure and should be discontinued is both facile and un-nuanced. To do so is to ignore the ideas, learning, and analyses of the people who know aid's impacts directly by being on the recipient side of assistance. This book, therefore, is not for people who want to end international assistance. It is not for isolationists or for cynics. The very fact that people in aid-receiving societies can, with clear eyes, criticize much of what aid now does—and at the same time express their confidence that the system can change—means that they still believe aid can be an effective force for progress in their societies and the larger world.

What this Book Is; Who this Book Is Intended for

Everyone who works in the international aid enterprise can benefit from hearing the ideas and analyses from people who live in aid-recipient countries. Most especially, people on the receiving side of assistance want the donors of international aid and the large international assistance agencies that operate in their countries to hear what they have to say.

Beyond these two groups who are directly involved in providing aid, the experiences and ideas of people in aid-recipient societies should interest any individual who writes an annual check to a favorite charity and all public donors who want to know if the taxes they spend on foreign assistance are doing any good. Legislators who are beholden to these taxpayers as they allocate national funds and set the rules and regulations that govern foreign assistance would also benefit by listening to the perspectives of those who receive these funds and feel the effects of the rules and regulations. And policy makers of international and multinational bodies can learn useful lessons about the longer-term impacts of their deliberations and decisions, impacts that are felt by people in distant parts of the world.

The international aid enterprise is large and growing in terms of the numbers of actors, and it embraces a broad range of public and private agencies and personnel. It includes the many-layered apparatus of multilateral and bilateral donor agencies; multinational, national, and local organizations; academics; private foundations; and corporations. It includes the staffs (and possibly their spouses and their children!) who work in all these agencies at all these levels. Finally, it involves, at some level, citizens in countries across the globe who take up the challenge of providing assistance across borders.

The experiences reported here—especially as they show consistent patterns across locations and over time—are reminders of challenges aid providers should not ignore. The insights of aid recipients provide a strong analytical base for understanding how and why problems persist. And, the confidence many express that things could be done differently and better (more efficiently and more effectively) pushes everyone in the aid system to take the steps necessary to change it.

Some Clarification of Terminology

Two additional points will help readers understand how to interpret the material that follows.

First, although within the international assistance community we use the terminology of "donors" and "implementing agencies" to distinguish among actors, many people in receiving countries conflate these categories. They use the term "donors" to refer to outside funding sources of any type that, because they provide resources, also shape the policy and programming context of assistance. When people in receiving countries are quoted as speaking of "donors," they may be referring to international NGOs or to bilateral or multilateral donor agencies. In the following text, we use either their term "donors" or, more often, the term "aid providers" when discussing those on the giving side of international aid.

Second, in choosing quotations from our many conversations to illustrate the issues raised, we have conscientiously chosen those that represent large numbers of people. In some cases, we quote an individual who stated a widely shared viewpoint with special clarity. In other cases, a comment was made so frequently that the writers of the field visit reports referred to it with language such as "many people said" or "a number of people felt." In both uses, we name the country from which the quotation came. When we can, we identify something about the individual who said it. Where many people used the same or similar language, we do not try to identify the characteristics of all the people who made the point.

International Assistance in a Larger Context

The "international assistance" we discuss is clearly only one aspect of the interaction between poor and rich countries. International aid for development, peace, and human rights can contribute to, but does not determine, their achievement. Foreign policies, trade policies, private sector initiatives, and markets all play roles that can reinforce or contradict aid efforts, and vice versa. Although the Listening Project conversations invited people to discuss all aspects of international efforts to be helpful, the majority focused on small-scale project interventions of international and local non-governmental organizations. Most focused on humanitarian or development assistance, some also on conflict resolution or environmental interventions.

That the majority of conversations turned to people's immediate experiences is understandable. Many commented on the distance they feel from high-level decision-makers in the international assistance apparatus. Nonetheless, many also described how even these distant decisions and policies affect their lives. In a very real sense, they understand the multiple levels of international factors that affect their lives and, in the conversations reported here, take responsibility for addressing those that they feel they can influence to achieve the social, political, and economic progress they want.

How this Book Is Organized

The power of people's common experience is reported in the chapters that follow. To ground the evidence, Chapter 2 provides fuller details about the Listening Project and its methodology, including a discussion of the challenges of listening to and hearing what people really mean. Chapter 3 reports what people say about the cumulative impacts of aid efforts. It tells a layered story that differentiates between what many see as the positive (but sometimes marginal, insignificant, or negative) immediate tangible effects of assistance and what they see as negative intangible effects that accumulate over multiple experiences and years of international assistance. Chapter 4 analyzes how and why these effects occur, noting that steps the international assistance community has taken to improve efficiency and effectiveness in the delivery of assistance (increasingly relying on business principles) introduce intrinsic contradictions between aid's intent and its outcomes. In Chapter 5, we examine how the agendas aid providers develop outside aid-receiving contexts can have unintended, sometimes negative, consequences, and in Chapter 6, we look at how the operational procedures aid-providing agencies employ to ensure attention to basic values can inadvertently reinforce the intangible negative impacts aid recipients say they experience.

The next four chapters delve in more detail into four issues that people in aid-recipient societies consistently raise, issues that are particularly challenging for international assistance agencies. These are partnerships (Chapter 7), corruption and waste (Chapter 8), communication (Chapter 9), and participation (Chapter 10).

Finally, we conclude by reviewing the evidence from aid recipients' experiences and examining the immediate implications for how aid providers (donors and operational agencies) should change aspects of their work. We revisit the fundamental goals of international assistance as an enterprise and suggest that, given the broad evidence reported here, the enterprise faces a decisive moment.

The Power of Cumulative Evidence

Every day, smart and dedicated people who care about the world get on airplanes and fly to distant locations. Their hope and intent is to help people overcome poverty, resolve conflict, save and restore the environment, and achieve basic human rights. An elaborate apparatus of agencies, funding mechanisms, and legislative choices recruits, funds, supports, and enables the work of these individuals. The international assistance community spans all borders and represents a valued solidarity, generosity, and concern for others.

At the same time, every day, smart and determined people in distant locations receive these people and their efforts to be helpful in the forms of funding, programs and projects, advocacy campaigns, and partnerships. Many in receiving locations also devote their time, energy, and work to the programs international assistance supports.

In spite of the energies and efforts of both givers and receivers, many on both sides see that aid has many flaws. Throughout the Listening Project, we heard many aid providers say: "None of this is new." "We've heard it all before." "You can never please everyone." "It is better to do some good than to do nothing." "Nothing is perfect." Readers of this book may be tempted to fall into this litany as well. Much of what we report here may sound familiar. But, it isn't.

The power of this book is in the *cumulative* evidence it reports. When so many people in so many places, people who have experienced different forms of assistance from many different international providers, still come up with essentially the same message, this goes beyond the localized griping of some people. Across very different contexts, people described their experiences with very different aid providers in remarkably similar terms. Their analyses of why and how things go wrong are common and consistent. When they judge how aid, as a system, has "added up" in their societies, the overwhelming majority cite negative cumulative effects.

This cumulative evidence demands attention. If one could ever justify continuing to provide aid in the usual ways in the face of familiar repeated criticisms—as so many aid providers do—it should be impossible to do so with the cumulative voice of aid recipients in our ears. Fortunately, these voices not only criticize what has been done, but also provide clear indicators of what can, and must, be done to make aid work. People in recipient societies want aid efforts to be successful. If the international assistance enterprise is to become the tool for social, political, and economic progress that many wish, it behooves providers of aid to listen to them.

• • • • • • • • •

CHAPTER TWO

THE CHALLENGES OF LISTENING: HOW DO WE HEAR AND UNDERSTAND WHAT PEOPLE REALLY MEAN?

... in which we describe the challenges the Listening Project faced in gathering the evidence of this book and the methods used to deal with these challenges.

> 66 There is a responsibility for foreigners to quiet their voice. Calm down and visit and get to know the people. Don't run in with your own agenda. 99
>
> - Monk on the Thai-Burma border

Throughout the Listening Project, those of us involved as listeners asked ourselves three questions. First, "Are we hearing anything new, or are we simply eliciting a series of concerns and complaints—some valid and some simply uninformed—we have heard before?" Second, "How do we weigh different people's comments; how do we sort the significant and wise from the superficial, whining and biased?" And third, "How many times do we need to hear people saying something to recognize its importance?"

These are not insignificant questions. Listening is challenging. It takes time and energy, it demands attention and receptiveness, and it requires choices. Listening at both the interpersonal level and the broader, societal level is a discipline that involves setting aside expectations of what someone will say and opening up, instead, to the multiple levels at which humans communicate with each other.

At the interpersonal level, one needs first to be quiet long enough to let the other person talk (a practice that is difficult for some of us!). Then one needs to ask questions and probe the ideas offered rather than interject one's own opinions and analyses or jump to quick conclusions about what the other person means. A listening conversation is distinct from an interview. It opens space for dialogue on issues of importance to both parties. The act of listening is a way of showing respect.

> " I would propose [to my work team] that, although we conduct participatory monitoring and evaluation for all our projects, now more than ever I have realized that numbers are irrelevant because you can't read people's feelings through them. And feelings are particular to each person. I think the process of the Listening Project is enlightening, because it's often difficult to just listen, because I usually butt in with my own perceptions and opinions. But sometimes, in order to really understand the other person's feelings and perceptions, it's important just to listen to them. "
>
> - Listening Team member, Solomon Islands

At the broader, society-wide level, listening takes on additional dimensions. To listen to a large number and range of people across cultures and societies, often through translation, magnifies the challenges. The Listening Project faced a series of decisions as we crossed the sometimes large chasms of language, culture, experience, and viewpoint. We had to decide to whom we would listen, how many people to include, how to record their ideas and opinions, how to be sure—as sure as we could be—that we really understood what they were saying. Finally, we had to decide which ideas were valid and useful to the questions the Listening Project was seeking to answer. As one Listening Team member noted, "We are hearing many things about the work that we do. We need to analyze together with the recipients what matters most."

It is only fair that the authors of this book describe the challenges we faced, because how we handled them influences what we report in this book. In this chapter, we outline the specific dilemmas of listening that the Listening Project encountered, and we explain how we chose to address them. Knowing what approaches and criteria we found useful will provide a basis for readers to judge and interpret the ideas presented in this book.

Specific Dilemmas of Listening Faced by the Listening Project

The first and most obvious challenge we faced was the broad range of disagreements, contradictions, and inconsistencies in people's ideas within and across countries. What should we do with these? Should we report them, select among them, or try to resolve them?

Second, because some people (and some Listening Exercise reports) are much more articulate than others, they excite us when others lose our attention. We always want to quote the clever conversations! Does this mean that these people are smart and correct? Or does it merely mean that they have facility with words?

Third, there are always people who like to complain. How much complaining do we need to listen to? How seriously do we need to take these complaints? Do they tell us things we need to know and address?

Fourth, some people clearly have more knowledge and experience than others. Does this mean that they also have more understanding? How should we judge the relationship between experience and insight? Should we weigh some comments as more worthy than others if the speaker convinces us of his or her depth of knowledge?

Fifth, and related to number four, we knew we would encounter people with different interests and biases based on social standing, group affiliations, and personal background. How should we differentiate between special insight gained because of such perspectives and self-interested bias that distorts perspectives and provides marginal insight?

Sixth, a dilemma that grows from working through translation is important. When we hear apparent agreement across contexts with many people using similar words to offer an idea, are these people really expressing the same ideas or are the translators "packaging" many ideas under certain familiar phrases? When the discourse is peppered with humanitarian or development or human rights jargon, does this language convey people's true ideas or are they using words they think we expect and like?

And finally, we acknowledge that we have our own biases—our own "favorite" issues and ideas. How are we to guard against listening favorably to the voices of those with whom we agree and discounting the ideas that are less appealing or less intriguing?

Recognizing these challenges, we knew we needed to follow a rigorous process of listening to all ideas. We know from experience that qualitative evidence can be rigorous when systematically analyzed by many experienced and thoughtful people working together. So, we developed systems, and layers of systems, to gather, sift through, sort, and analyze the ideas and the evidence that people offered. We describe these systems here.

Listening with Aid Providers

The Listening Project was rooted in CDA's collaborative learning methodology, a methodology tested over many years with aid workers from many different contexts. The listening and collaborative learning process is evidence-based and inductive. We do not formulate a theory or hypothesis before we gather evidence. We go to the field recognizing that there is an enormous amount of experience and knowledge in aid-recipient societies and among aid providers which should be heard.

By involving many local and international staff of both local and international aid agencies in the listening, and by engaging them also in sorting through the vast field-based evidence, we were able to hear more, to add layers to a deeper and more systematic analysis, and, with them, to deliberate and weigh the critiques and recommendations aid recipients offered.

We also knew that involving the very people who are the aid providers in listening to aid recipients could set up a biased process. To mitigate the possibility that aid recipients would shape their answers to please the aid providers, the Listening Project took care in composing and assigning the Listening Teams. First, we put listeners from different aid agencies together on each of the field teams. Second, as much as possible, team members were sent to communities where they do not normally work. Third, when appropriate, we mixed teams by gender, language capability, and background.

For many of the aid agency staff, the chance to listen with colleagues to a range of people was a rare and valued exercise and an opportunity to learn and share in an openly critical way. A Listening Team member in the Solomon Islands shared a common sentiment: "The Listening Project has been really helpful and really built my confidence as an NGO officer. The peer-to-peer approach taken in this exercise relaxes people to talk openly and freely about their opinions. Joining LP makes me realize that as NGO workers, we talk a lot and never listen. This teaches us to take another approach: talk and listen."

Listening Broadly and Systematically

The basic questions of the Listening Project were open-ended and broad, guided by a genuine interest in learning about how recipients feel about aid and a commitment to improving aid's effectiveness. The Listening Teams asked people in recipient communities the following questions: *What has been your personal experience with international assistance efforts? What approaches did you find useful or effective—and which not? How do you analyze and assess the positive and negative effects of international assistance efforts in your community and your society, over time and cumulatively? What do you suggest should be done differently and by whom?*

These questions are not the typical substance of conversations between aid providers and recipients. More often, as donors and aid workers visit field sites, they initially ask about needs. Often they use questionnaires or standard interview protocols to gather demographic data (sometimes to provide a baseline for later evaluation). In field visits after project activities are under way, staff usually meet with "beneficiaries" to discuss the specifics of what their agencies are doing—does the well provide water, is the training useful, did the seeds arrive on time, and so on.

In contrast, unscripted listening conversations invite people to take a step back, encouraging them to reflect on their experiences and their observations and, using this evidence, to bring up whatever issues matter most to them. Listening Teams explored whatever themes and issues about international assistance people raised, engaging them in further analysis by asking many follow-up questions, such as: "Why is this important? Why do you think this or that happened? How does your experience differ from the experience of others in your community?" We actively sought recommendations and engaged people in critical thinking about what could and should be done differently (and by whom) to address the concerns they raised.

To address the challenges of listening openly, we worked closely with and mentored the local and international aid agency staff recruited to join the Listening Teams. Many told us that they were unsure how to broach the broad topics of the Listening Project and how to follow up on any ideas beyond their area of expertise or comfort zone. Some said they were fearful of such open-endedness, and some worried about raising expectations in the communities they visited. A few questioned the very premise behind the need to invite critical reflections and feedback on past aid efforts. Each Listening Exercise, therefore, began with a one- to two-day orientation for the listeners to help them become comfortable with and develop the skills for open-ended and far-ranging conversations about the cumulative effects of international assistance.

Two to four facilitators provided by the Listening Project led this workshop in each country to prepare Listening Teams to engage in unscripted, inquiring, and respectful conversations. Listeners were then assigned to smaller teams to visit locations in particular regions, under the direction of one of these team leaders, for four to five days of conversations with local people. One team often stayed back to hold conversations with key interlocutors in the capital city. Most visits at the community level were unannounced, and conversations often occurred at random. The team would go to a village or town, split into two-person sub-teams, and simply ask people if they would be willing to talk. Conversations occurred sometimes in a tea shop, sometimes in a field or workplace, and sometimes in individual homes and gardens. Some teams made appointments to visit government officials, civil society organizations, or business people who worked in offices. Listeners always went in twos, with one person engaging directly in the conversation while the other took notes, allowing them to discuss later what they had heard and observed. When translation was needed (largely for expatriates or due to regional dialects), there were often three on a team. Listening teams took detailed notes of the conversations, but did not tape record them because most people were not comfortable with being recorded.

Collaboratively Analyzing and Reflecting on What People Said

The groups of listeners in each region of the country met daily to discuss what they were hearing. The focus of these debriefings was on ensuring that listeners could truly discern what people had said and reflecting on it. Often these discussions involved Listening Team members asking each other to repeat the actual words of the person they were quoting and, then, discussing for some time how best to capture the real meaning the person intended. Through these discussions, many of the team members learned to recognize and correct their own biases and to hear, more carefully, what people had really said. These meetings also provided a means to sort out (mis)interpretations that came through language translation. When several local team members would hear the words and interpret them, the precision of translation increased.

When the Listening Teams had completed conversations in the regions, they came back together for a day or two to do a collective analysis of what they all had heard and to reflect on it. Again, the challenges of emphasis and interpretation arose. Sometimes, teams had heard different things determined by the locations they visited and the types of international assistance people had experienced in those areas. Sometimes, differences seemed to come from the backgrounds and priorities of the Listening Teams themselves—some focused their questions and conversations around their own interests (gender, agricultural development, health issues, etc.), while others were more open-ended in their explorations. In these joint analysis sessions, listeners—many of them local people—also added their own experiences with, and judgments of, international assistance. The challenge in these collective sessions was to find the composite voice of people without submerging minority viewpoints or losing subtlety and nuance.

When the Listening Teams completed the joint analysis, the team leader wrote a "field visit report," which was then returned for comments by all listeners who were involved in the Listening Exercise. Once the feedback was in, the reports were finalized, translated into the national language (or more than one in some cases), and circulated more widely in country and globally.[1]

The Listening Project was committed to hearing all voices. We valued the common themes as well as the outliers; we wanted to gather ideas and insights from people at all levels of the societies that had been on the receiving end of assistance, as well as to listen to the analyses of Listening Team members and others who were themselves engaged in providing assistance. Thus, the reports that came from each country included summaries both of what Listening Teams had heard in the field as well as reflections on the Listening Teams' discussions and analyses. As the material from individual country visits mounted, complexities also mounted. More pages of notes and reports meant more ideas and opinions.

---

[1] A list of the Field Visits is in Appendix 1. The Field Visit Reports and translations can be downloaded under the Listening Project section of the CDA website at www.cdainc.com.

When multiple Listening Exercise field visit reports were complete, the Listening Project convened groups of experienced practitioners—most of them aid providers—to read and analyze the reports. These sessions were intended to gather additional insights from aid providers, as well as to begin the sorting, sifting, and judging of themes and issues. In addition, Listening Project staff developed a series of "Issue Papers" that highlighted themes where broad agreement, or broad disagreement, occurred across countries and types of assistance (listed in Appendix 3). These papers became the focus of sixteen "Feedback Workshops" the Listening Project organized (listed in Appendix 1), intending again to increase the number of people (and brains!) who examined the evidence and analyzed the importance of different ideas and insights.

Analyzing the Cumulative Voice

The authors of this book worked with all of this material: raw field notes capturing thousands of individual conversations, field visit reports where Listening Teams consolidated and highlighted the themes and reflections from their given country experiences, reports from the series of Feedback Workshops where aid professionals and others had together read and reflected on the Listening Exercise reports and Issue Papers, and our own experiences in the field facilitating Listening Exercises. Our job was to listen for the cumulative voice of those who live in societies that have received international assistance, further explicated by the multiple reflections of other people who had taken the time and effort also to listen through Feedback Workshops and consultations, and to assemble it so that it would be instructive, challenging, and usable to improve the impacts of international assistance.

Even with all of this careful and intelligent filtering by the many layers of people who dealt with the evidence gathered in different contexts (Listening Teams in each country, Feedback Workshops, reports, issue papers), the authors faced choices. To guard against the pitfalls outlined in the questions at the beginning of this chapter, we followed several additional steps.

First, we maintained the commitment to listen widely. The importance of listening across societies and geographical regions; across levels of experience, social settings, gender and age groups; and across spheres of work, income, and educational levels was obvious in the gathering of ideas. This breadth of representation "corrected" for any particularities of experience, social context, or bias. As we wrote the findings, we again examined this breadth. Where themes and commonalities appeared among all the groups, we concluded that there is validity to individual expressions around such ideas.

Second, each of the authors read and re-read (multiple times) all of the field visit reports, Feedback Workshop reports, and a broad range of the individual field notes. Experience shows that one, two, or three readings do not necessarily tell us what people mean. After multiple times of "listening" to the same people through these re-readings, at some point, we begin to sense the texture and rhythm of their voices, which then lets us "hear" them more accurately. As far as one can from reading, we immersed ourselves into their context and circumstances, which then helped us to hear their voices and learn what they meant us to learn.

Third, we met with each other multiple times to delve into each Listening Exercise report and to read across all field visit reports on every given issue, "arguing" out our varying interpretations. The rigor we forced on each other as we questioned why we thought people meant one thing or another, and the frequent return to the texts and notes of conversations to see what else could be learned, regularly moved us beyond our first impressions and helped simplistic conclusions progress to much more subtlety.

The process of working with these many voices has sometimes been dull, but more often, it was enlightening. The moments when we think we "have it" only to discover that some other point is raised in a given sentence that may alter what we first heard are actually exciting ones. The testing of each other to see where our own biases shaped conclusions is fun.

These were the processes that we adopted to work with the rich material synthesized in this book. The chapters that follow report the issues that people raised across the various contexts, as well as their shared judgments and ideas for change.

A Note on People's Reactions to the Listening Project Approach

Because the very act of listening in this open-ended way and the intentionality of the methods the Listening Project used were new for many aid providers and recipients, a number of them commented on their experiences either as a member of a Listening Team or as a recipient community person talking to a Listening Team.

The vast majority of people welcomed the Listening Teams and were very generous with their time. At the end of listening conversations, people often expressed "appreciation for the opportunity to talk freely" and for the time that Listening Teams took to listen to them. Many said that it was the first time they had been invited to speak so openly and freely; usually they had been asked only to talk about their involvement in a specific project or activity. Some also expressed hope that their opinions and ideas would be shared with providers in the chain of decision-making and planning of assistance programs, in other words, with the people who can change the way the work is done. One young person in Mali exclaimed, "Please make sure to take good notes of what we are saying!"

Many times across many locales, we were impressed by people's interest in learning what had been discussed in other regions. They were eager to compare and, where relevant, to learn from others' experiences and/or to provide advice to them. Many invited Listening Teams to return for more conversations.

"The donors never take the time to consult with and listen to beneficiaries. This is the first time I have seen that!" (Female President of an association, Mali)

"We are happy with this [Listening] Exercise to tell the stories of NGOs to people outside." (Dominican sister working as a project director, Philippines)

"Our international friends said they would serve, but they didn't, so there is a distance between them and my people. People now realize they are not here to help. No one is listening to us and we want to express our views." (Librarian, Afghanistan)

"All this while, organizations came only to take a head-count. You are the only people who have come and listened to our problems." (Elderly man in an IDP camp, Sri Lanka)

"Thank you for listening to us and allowing us to tell you what we would like to tell those who have power over this great power that is international cooperation." (Afro-Ecuadorian woman, Ecuador)

For their part, most Listening Team members found the listening methodology practical, useful, and refreshing because it was "without heavy protocol requirements or survey tools," as one local facilitator said. They appreciated opportunities to listen to people in communities outside their implementation sites and to hear their experiences (and compare them to their own project sites). Many said they were excited to be given the time to engage in such open conversations and reflections. Many said they were changed by the experience of hearing the complexity and subtlety of people's voices.

"For four days I was a student, and all the people were my teachers." (Listening Team member, Philippines)

"I've heard the stories, I've learned from them, and now I want to spend more time asking questions than giving answers ....We have always done monitoring using complicated formats and, while this Listening Project compares to be the simplest exercise, it proves itself to be a vital tool that should be used to communicate effectively with rural communities. I have noticed that taking the LP approach, people are not reserved and it could be because of the informal set-up that comes with LP." (Listening team member, Solomon Islands)

"We are in a failing business if we are looking to understand and document only things that are projectized and immediately observable. We are missing the larger picture of development." (Staff of a large international NGO, United States)

"I don't know of another systematic effort to listen to the people, to learn of the experience the people in the communities have with external aid. I see this Listening Exercise as being very interesting .... I did not expect to hear such clear reflections that in a way show us the level of understanding that the people of the communities have on the subject of cooperation and external aid." (NGO Staff, Ecuador)

• • • • • • • • •

CHAPTER THREE

THE CUMULATIVE IMPACTS OF INTERNATIONAL ASSISTANCE

... in which we report what people say about the "impacts" of international assistance, which they call "changes," "results," or "effects." The story is often cheerful in the short term, but becomes more challenging over the long run as aid project after aid project comes and goes. This review of aid recipients' commentary sets the stage for considering how the international aid enterprise has increasingly organized itself.

The Listening Project asked people who live in countries that receive international assistance to assess the cumulative impacts of this aid on their societies. People said this was an unusual request. They were used to being asked about specific projects and programs. To answer the larger and longer-term question of how these multiple projects and programs add up over time, they reflected not only on their own direct experience but also on the effects of aid efforts on others and on their societies' overall prospects.

What People Expect from Aid

As they judge the effects of international assistance on their lives and societies, people focus on whether the changes they experience are positive (vs. negative), whether they are significant (vs. minor), and whether they are lasting (vs. temporary). What people want is significant positive and lasting change. What they expect is that international assistance should contribute to this kind of change, and they name specifically three areas where they think this support should focus.

1. Economic Betterment

People want and expect international assistance to improve their current and/or future economic prospects. How they judge aid's impacts depends on whether or not it increases the likelihood of a secure livelihood. Roads that open markets, water that allows improved crops, schooling and training that lead to employment or productive skills, and even housing that can be used for commercial purposes are welcomed. Recipients assess the benefit of assets provided through aid—seeds, tools, boats, and even loans—according to whether they lead to greater economic security.

2. Improved Political and Security Conditions

Although improvements in economic well-being are most important, many people also talk about the influences of international assistance on their political and social conditions. They look for, and hope for, aid providers to have positive impacts on their governance structures and on their physical safety. When the assistance supports new ways of engaging with their government or improvements in their safety, they welcome it. People want aid providers to support them in gaining voice *vis a vis* their government. They welcome support for their efforts to reduce mistrust and conflicts.

"Skill training is better than receiving goods. We increase our income, it helps us become more creative, we have more choices for our livelihood, and we can use the profits to buy other things we need such as rice, food and medicine." (Woman at a roadside stand, Cambodia)

Nearly every person, group, or government official talked about the need to achieve sustainable livelihoods and economic development. Some felt that most of the money given to Bosnia should have been spent on developing the local economy and that if more had been invested in job creation, they would not be so dependent on international aid now. Many said that if they had good jobs, they could have returned and rebuilt houses on their own and wished that money had been put into the economy instead of house construction. (Listening Project Report, Bosnia-Herzegovina)

Communities in all regions seemed to be in agreement that livelihoods and job creation were by far the most critical area of support by development actors wishing to leave a lasting, positive footprint. (Listening Project Report, Thailand)

Many who received training commented that their farming efforts are now "more efficient and sustainable." As one person said, "the trained people are here and they are educating the community. The knowledge will pass from generation to generation." (Listening Project Report, Ethiopia)

Many people said they did not want any more gifts of goods, but rather, they needed training, agricultural implements, seeds, fertilizer, and other forms of support so they could seek employment and grow their own food more effectively. As one person put it, "the help we are getting is for today only." (Listening Project Report, Angola)

"Our circumstances have improved a lot with the signing of the MOU between the Indonesian government and the GAM (the Acehnese independence movement). And this happened partly because of the large international presence after the tsunami. The international presence created a pitch for peace; the international presence supports peace." (Group of men, Aceh, Indonesia)

People want self-reliance and to focus on long-term development and planning after they have awareness and training. People talked about how project timeframes are too short and long-term projects with community involvement in needs assessments, planning, and evaluation are necessary. People want "know-how" before they receive aid. They want to be able to figure things out and to assess their problems for themselves, rather than having NGOs tell the people the issues they face. (Listening Project Report, Myanmar/Burma)

Many people expressed a desire to see the faces and know the feelings of the people giving them aid and to better understand their motivations. The repeated requests to have more outsiders present reflected a desire for agencies to build relationships of mutual respect and humanize each other. (Listening Project Report, Cambodia)

3. A Sense of Solidarity, Colleagueship, and Support

Many people say that they want a sense of connectedness to people in other parts of the world. They welcome the expressions of solidarity that international assistance brings. When aid providers discuss problems and solutions with them and suggest new ideas or new ways of doing things, they see these as expressions of caring and colleagueship.

What People Say They Get from International Aid

> ❝Without aid, we could not survive, and there would be no life in Kosovo. It is not fair to say that no difference was made; but what was possible was not exactly what was done. ❞
>
> - Government official, Kosovo

Not surprisingly, people differ in their judgments about the effects of various assistance programs and projects. Some attribute improved economic, social, and political security to aid efforts and point to specific ways that solidarity and colleagueship of international assistance actors have supported them or people they know. Others feel that they have made no personal progress in any of these spheres and question the effectiveness of international assistance, saying, "Change? What change? There has been no change!" Specific aid efforts have clearly worked for some people and not for others.

Positives Are Specific

As the introduction to this book noted, most people feel that international aid is a good thing. They are glad it exists and want it to continue. Many tell positive stories about specific projects, individual staff, or special planning or decision-making processes that they credit with achieving what they hoped for. Some of the positive impacts are lasting, such as when a road improves access to a market or women develop skills that they feel improve their families' lives.

"With all the international aid that came, we are really thankful because even though we are here, far from them, we appreciate that they think of us. If we were to personally see them, we would hug them out of happiness." (Local health worker, Philippines)

"People in my village are very grateful for the road because now with trucks coming into our village, the women can take their vegetables to the market. Before, the tomatoes just rotted in the gardens. Tomatoes go bad quickly, and despite our attempts in the past to take them to the market to sell, we always lost." (Woman, Solomon Islands)

"It saved our lives. I simply don't know where to start, to whom to say thank you." (A person in Kosovo)

Cumulative Effects Are Largely Negative

However, as people analyze the longer term and society-wide effects of international assistance, the negative impacts seem to outweigh the positive ones. The particular benefits they experience from any specific aid program can, they say, be compromised by how aid is provided. The consistency of views from people across all regions and social strata of countries, and across all the countries where the Listening Project went, was striking. Everywhere people described markedly similar experiences with the processes of assistance and explained how these processes undermined the very goals of the assistance. This consistency deserves detailed explanation.

1. Although people want economic support, they see that aid increases dependency and powerlessness.

People do not want to need assistance! They do not want to depend on outsiders for help. Even in emergencies, as they express their grateful surprise at the generosity of international aid, many say that it would be better for aid to address the longer-term challenges that cause their crises. Many people say that too much aid is given both in emergencies and over the long-term, causing people to believe, as one senior Afghan Ministry official said, that "the money spigot and the large budgets are permanent."

In addition, when assistance continues over many years, some people begin to question its motives. They see that international actors bring projects that, instead of solving a problem, seem only to lead to more projects and more assistance, *ad infinitum*. When assistance is provided in "dribs and drabs," as a Zimbabwean village chief said, and when it arrives in piecemeal projects with short time frames (as many people said), it has no lasting effect except to create expectations—and a need—for yet another follow-up project, yet more assistance, and yet more outsiders deciding what should be done and how they will do it. "Too much" and "too easy" are how many people explain why aid produces dependency.

Some connect their dependency on outsiders to a growing sense of powerlessness. They say it is disempowering to "feel used" in activities others design and run. Further, they feel that the ways that aid agencies interact with them diminishes their power to manage their own lives, which undermines their capabilities and self-confidence.

Competition among the aid-providing agencies also feeds into people's sense that "someone else is in control." When an aid agency positions itself as being more successful than other agencies for funding or publicity reasons, it claims ownership of the activities it funds rather than ensuring that people own them. People say they are encouraged to "participate" in projects designed and managed by outsiders where they have no control.

Paying Attention to the "Messages" of Aid

The arrival of what appear to be abundant resources in a resource-scarce environment conveys the positive message that "people care." But it also says: "you don't have to worry—aid agencies have resources and plans to feed you, build your houses, set up a clinic for you, etc." When agencies are seen to do needs assessments to decide where to focus their aid and when aid providers interview people asking "what do you need?" the dual message is that the more you need, the more you will get and that whatever you need, you will get.

> ❝ The [international] intervention to restore law and order after the violence took the steam out of domestic efforts to do things. Support for civil society weakened because people felt they didn't have to do it now. Everyone is glad that happened, but there was a downside to it because it took the stuffing out of homegrown attempts to deal with the insurgency and we are still trying to get over this. ❞
>
> - Consultant, Solomon Islands

Fundamentally, people say, the message conveyed when assistance comes is that they will be provided for until real development occurs. The message is that they are objects, not subjects, of assistance. Cumulatively, over time, international assistance—as it is now given—engenders passivity and undermines initiative. People in many places feel that aid feeds dependency and powerlessness.

"There was too much assistance too fast, and international agencies should be slower in their distribution. People should help themselves first and only request and receive assistance when they cannot help themselves. By giving out so easily, you are turning them into beggars. Some villages received too much to stop and think of the value of all the things they have been given." (Policeman, Thailand)

"This food assistance ought to stop. This money should be given to infrastructure development. Seventy-five percent of families in this village receive rations for food each month but are unable to pull themselves out of poverty. Changes will be there definitely if families take their economic development into their hands." (Villager, Sri Lanka)

"We don't want to be controlled by the NGOs. We want to work together when necessary, but not all the time. We want to be independent ... We feel like they tell us what to do ...This is because they think the CBOs [community-based organizations] don't have enough capacity ... In order to empower refugees, they need to support them. When they don't do this, they disempower us." (A refugee and staff of a local NGO, Thai-Burma border)

"There is a lot of dependency syndrome in the community. Families are continuously depicting situations of poverty so that they can be given assistance ... There is a feeling that donors want to keep their jobs, hence, they don't want to do poverty eradication programs, but those that are short-term so that the community remains dependent on them." (Woman, Kenya)

"It's unavoidable that humanitarian aid created a situation where we are programmed to receive. If aid wasn't just given, but if there was a program that was much more of a give and take, it would be more beneficial for the whole community.... It's important not to get things for free so that people are not programmed to get aid. If you give it for free, you take away the sense of responsibility they had."
(Karen leader, Thai-Burma border)

One truth about external aid that occasionally presents itself is a double dependency ... whereas grassroots people can develop a dependency on NGOs and other supportive entities, the NGOs in turn become dependent on grassroots leaders and groups. They need them to launch their projects, bring out the people, generate enthusiasm in the participants, and finally, to demonstrate to supervisors, donors, and visitors their achievements, or at least that the projects are underway. Their positions, salaries, and sense of efficiency are all linked to the cooperation and conformity of the aid recipients. The situation affords a certain level of power to the people and their leaders in their relationships and negotiations with the NGOs, but only if they are conscious of the needs and desires of these institutions. (Listening Project Report, Ecuador)

2. Although people want improved security and political stability, they see that aid can worsen conflict and increase tensions among groups.

Many countries where aid is given have experienced wide-scale violence, sometimes over extended periods. In every location where the Listening Project visited, people talked about the effects of international assistance on the likelihood of conflict in their areas. In all but one country, people said that international aid over time had introduced or reinforced tensions among groups and that, cumulatively, it had increased the potential for violence and/or fundamental divisions within their societies.

"Many committees for different projects of different organizations are formed, and people are divided according to who belongs to which organization." (Staff of a local NGO, Burma/Myanmar)

"Ex-UNITA soldiers should not be given expensive cows as reintegration aid if we don't get anything, too. Don't distinguish between villagers—we all suffer. We all have the same problems. We are all community members. If an ex-combatant needs salt, I need salt also."
(Woman in a village where soldiers were being repatriated, Angola)

The categorization of people along ethnic lines (and resulting targeting of aid) often created tensions between refugees and domiciles (those who did not flee during the war), and even among different groups of returnees. Some people are bitter about this because they feel that the international community has reinforced ethnic differences.
(Listening Project Report, Bosnia-Herzegovina)

"I feel jealous. I don't know why NGOs help [the refugee village] and not our village. The refugee village has electricity; the road is better there, and here it is muddy. It makes me feel they are better than us."
(A male in a village next to refugee returnees, Cambodia)

"There is a flawed impression that peacebuilding is new, coming from outside. It is as if we are presented with somebody else's framework and need to adapt it. There are local ways to do this work, and people are capable to take it into their hands. What needs to be supported by outsiders is capacity building and strengthening of communities and local governments." (Staff of a local peace and development initiative, Philippines)

> "All the conflict work had the same mind frame of doing dialogue. This was out of touch with what was needed on the ground. It has given conflict resolution and peacebuilding a bad name. People see it as an initiative that doesn't do what people need. Its meaning and intent have been hijacked. It's not culturally sensitive either.... A lot of peacebuilding work does not understand the local dynamics, and as a result, the intervention does not work. Conflict resolution paradigms may work for the cultures that produced them, but they don't fit here. We need to rethink it. For a while after the war, it was all about dialogue and reconstruction that was naïve. These people are from the same culture and still entered a war." (PhD student and consultant, Lebanon)

The negative impacts they described go beyond interpersonal jealousies (which, though they may be unpleasant or even dangerous, seldom escalate into broader violence). Many people saw international aid as feeding into deeper group-identity schisms—sometimes divisions that had caused wars in the past. They pointed out that outside assistance agencies frequently define target groups according to ethnicity, religion, age, or other societal characteristics that they believe represent special vulnerability. However, according to people within aid-receiving countries, these outside agencies often define these targets because of an external agenda, such as a commitment to support the government, promote the return of refugees, encourage multiethnic coexistence, demobilize soldiers, or achieve some other priority set by outsiders. When provision of aid follows such externally determined criteria, this can and often does reinforce receiving country social and political divisions.[2]

People say that for outsiders to avoid exacerbating conflict (and, even more importantly, to recognize opportunities to support existing systems that enable cooperation and joint problem solving), aid providers must learn about local political and social dynamics. They point out that prepackaged programs and techniques developed in one context translate badly into other local realities. Where schisms exist, international actors must consult with and listen to a range of local views. People observe that current project cycles and procedures do not allocate attention, time, or resources for such consultation. They identify the urgency to distribute resources on a schedule set by donors (often "too fast") as undermining opportunities for outsiders to understand local social and political dynamics and processes.

---

[2] This idea is also discussed in Mary B. Anderson, *Do No Harm: How Aid Can Support Peace—Or War* (Boulder, Colorado: Lynne Reinner, 1999.)

Even as they want/expect assistance to improve their chances of economic security, people also want it to improve their political stability and personal security. When aid actually worsens their situation, people feel that this happens because outsiders act without adequate consultation and analysis.

3. Although people want solidarity and colleagueship, they more often feel frustrated, mistrusted and disrespected by the way aid is provided.

Everywhere, people tell stories about aid agencies that came to their area, asked lots of questions, sometimes even discussed projects they could fund, and then disappeared. People in many locations describe their confusion, frustration, and disappointment when assistance they expect is not forthcoming. What they perceive as "broken promises" makes them mistrust aid providers and question the notion of international assistance more generally.

> 66 Villagers consistently expressed disappointment with outsiders for taking their time to ask questions and even make promises, only to never return or provide the promised aid. This contributed to speculations that aid was somehow misused or redirected, or that outsiders were not responsible and trustworthy. 99
>
> - Listening Project Report, Cambodia

Who would not be frustrated by a process where people seem to offer help and then disappear? People describe how these experiences, which clearly happen again and again, make them feel misused and misled. If they take the time to meet and answer questions, they believe that they should receive something in exchange. When no aid comes, they wonder how the information they gave is being used. People also say that aid providers often do not communicate clearly about decision-making processes, project plans, the selection of beneficiaries/participants, and actual results achieved—and that this leads people to speculate about what is being hidden and why.

"Some NGOs come here, gather information, and don't come back. People are frustrated. Other organizations follow in their steps, and people are no longer willing to engage in conversations." (Village woman, Sri Lanka)

"People like us are not mad, we are simply sad because they came and lied to us. They collected data about how many families, how many homes, but the water project never materialized. [Aid agencies] just pass through! They come here and then go back and ask for things in our name. They are misleading others with our name."
(Villagers in a remote area of Timor-Leste)

"Donors believe there is a lack of capacity and that outsiders have to transfer their skills ... lots of short-term people are hired from outside because donors tell the ministries to develop project cycle management, something that people in the ministries already know." (Government Ministry staff, Afghanistan)

We heard from people who felt that they were treated without much respect or consideration. Such treatment was an insult to their dignity.... A few people said that international agencies claim to be "partners" with their beneficiaries or local organizations, but then behave as the owners/bosses. One local NGO representative talked about walking out of a presentation by an international organization—she found it so arrogantly and condescendingly presented that she could not bear to stay. (Listening Project Report, Bosnia-Herzegovina)

Virtually every person mentioned the importance of the consultation process, and many people expressed frustration.... A staff member of a donor-funded peace and development initiative saw the lack of consultation ... as disrespectful. He and others considered regular stakeholder consultation a critical step in determining if a project needs to be redesigned or stopped altogether, noting how a number of projects in the past have not received input from the actual participants. A [government officer] commented that the NGOs are supposed to get clearance from them to work in the community, but instead, the NGOs go directly to the community, which makes them feel disrespected. He added, "Some of the NGOs don't give us importance because they look down on us." (Listening Project Report, Philippines)

"NGO and donor work should be of high quality. The British built roads and railroad tracks here decades ago, and these still function. We need more high-quality infrastructure like this, not more bad roads." (Farmer, Sri Lanka)

"Acceptance brings trust, and trust brings teamwork. If one of the two factors is lacking, the result is the work of only one set of brains." (Group of rural villagers, Ecuador)

The frustration and mistrust they feel, many say, feeds into a sense of being disrespected. They also tell stories of personal and institutional encounters with the international assistance community that feed disrespect. Sometimes international aid workers are arrogant and bossy. Sometimes they convey disrespect indirectly through processes that ignore or devalue existing capabilities, ideas, and indigenous institutions.

When outsiders deliver inappropriate items or training, when they deliver aid to the "wrong" people while bypassing some who deserve it, when recipients are "consulted" but see no evidence that their ideas are considered, when construction projects break down soon after completion, people say that aid is wasteful. But, more important are the frustration and disrespect that people feel because providers do not listen when they try to offer their ideas and experience. To feel that they know what could work (or not) and to have outsiders ignore their ideas and knowledge is galling and, they feel, fundamentally disrespectful.

> "NGOs and government made too many promises which did not eventuate. A lot of interviews were done in communities, but nothing was forthcoming. We were given high hopes that assistance will be coming. Days, months, years passed by, still no green light. We don't trust them anymore now."
> - Female community leader, Solomon Islands

Some people also see disrespect when the international aid system fails to relate to and support existing capacities in their societies. They resent an assumption that people who receive assistance have not thought of certain issues before or that they have no experience or ideas that can be useful in developing solutions to their problems.

An Exception! Focus on Women

People in some locations illustrate how international assistance can get it "right" by citing examples of processes and programming to improve the status of women. Women—and some men—told of experiences where an international program focusing on women led to economic benefits for both men and women. Some told how changed perceptions of women's roles and capacities also changed broader attitudes and social interactions. Although some people felt that it is inappropriate for external actors to interfere with local male/female relations, it was interesting how many people described positive benefits from programming aimed at women.

One possible interpretation of this appreciation is that in this area, international assistance agencies did recognize and focus on an existing, but internally undervalued, resource (women's abilities) and, through approaches and programming to encourage and enlarge its expression, not only built on women's capacities, but also helped men recognize and appreciate them. We return to this in a later chapter exploring the impacts of internationally driven policies and agendas on receiving societies.

> "We have gained skills in community mobilization and grassroots leadership because of our partnerships with international organizations!"
> (Leader of a local Muslim women's group, Sri Lanka)
>
> "Women's life changed a lot. Before we didn't have a rice mill, we had to make everything by hand and walk far for the water each day. Now we have a rice mill that we share, and people are healthier because the clinic is near. Also, during communal meetings, women are encouraged and invited to speak up and voice opinions." (A young woman, Cambodia)
>
> "There is a lot of support for women here, and there are many examples that demonstrate our success. Some women have gotten access to an irrigated perimeter to grow food. Others are taking literacy classes. We have seen the disappearance of polio and measles. There is the fight against malaria with bed nets. Prenatal and post-natal consultations take place. Deliveries are in clinics, and caesarean sections are done for free. Infants from birth to six months are monitored to see if they are well nourished. We have access to information about nutrition for newborns." (Members of a women's group, Mali)
>
> "As a woman I say that in the past, women were not taken into consideration, but after the emergency due to the flood, we have learned to become organized and we are now leaders. Personally, this formed and motivated me to become a leader." (Official of a women's federation, Bolivia)
>
> Some women commented that because of international assistance, more women were elected and got involved in government and the NGO sector. (Listening Project Report, Bosnia-Herzegovina)

How Important are Cumulative Impacts?

The consistency in the judgments of people across many contexts about how international aid "adds up" is instructive. Overall, people appreciate international assistance. They like both the idea of international support and, in many (but certainly not all) instances, the actual results of specific aid efforts. Even though people vary in their assessments of the effectiveness of individual projects and programs, the majority agree that the aid enterprise is important and that it should continue.

When asked to step back from particulars and to comment on how aid efforts add up over time, however, the judgments change in two important ways. First, assessments go from mixed to primarily negative. Second, they go from specific and tangible to broad and intangible.

> 66 We have to place more heart than technique in this thing called development, and [external] cooperation does not put heart into it. 99
>
> - A government staff person, Ecuador

Why might so many people in so many places weigh the relative importance of specific gains against broader effects in this way? The answer is found in people's attention to intangible as well as tangible impacts. When people feel that outsiders are making decisions about and for them rather than with them, when they feel others exert power over their lives, when they feel the disrespect this communicates—these feelings may mount over time. When their lives are not improving as rapidly as they wish (though they acknowledge that international assistance is not to blame), their frustration with what they see as the waste of immense resources—intended to help improve their lives—also increases over time. The query about cumulative impacts seems to elicit reflection on these intangible effects.

When they weigh the tangible and intangible impacts of international assistance, people report that the positive effects of even a much-needed road or water supply system provided through aid can be either reinforced or undermined by the processes of aid. In their experience, the impacts from how aid efforts are carried out are as significant to the long-term economic, social, and political outcomes from international aid efforts as the tangible things that aid delivers. They assess the impacts of assistance as a whole; they assess what was done and how successful it was in terms of lasting benefits and how it was done in terms of enabling people in the receiving society to exert increasing efficacy.

> "Before, everything was in our hands, but not now ... now they are not sharing information with us; this makes us feel like they are keeping us like workers only. We feel we are not respected, and it hurts our self-esteem. Before we made decisions together; now they dictate from outside. This was not our plan. We are like a puppet. Before we have ownership and make decisions; we know the situation ourselves. We wrote our own report before, not now. The NGOs come in and take over; we feel like we are nothing. I feel that this happens a lot—that the donors/NGOs take over ownership." (A local NGO leader, Thai-Burma border)

> "The feeling that we are worth less than those who come from outside has been penetrating and growing in the community through the power that the external actors impose." (Afro-Ecuadorian community leader, Ecuador)

> "Why don't you value local knowledge and capacity? We have engineers and experts, too." (Community member, Sri Lanka)

> "The differences in local and international salaries are insulting. You have internationals coming with huge salaries, but nationals probably do most of the work.... We need to revise our understanding of what we are worth. We have beautiful minds." (Government representative, Lebanon)

It is important to listen carefully to what people did and did not say.

When people named dependency and powerlessness as impacts of international assistance, they were not claiming that their societies were in all respects increasingly dependent and powerless. When they noted that aid contributes to intergroup tensions, they did not claim that they inevitably would therefore go into conflict. When they noted their frustration and sense of disrespect from the processes of international assistance efforts, they did not say that all aspects of their lives were frustrated. That is, people recognize that international assistance is an aspect, but only one aspect, of their reality.

The question then arises: How important are the intangible impacts that people identify? Also, how important are these impacts on development, peace, and good governance? These are questions that the findings of the Listening Project put squarely before the international assistance community.

Although people see international assistance as only one aspect of their lives, they nonetheless see this assistance as important enough to continue, and to try to change. They do not speak idly about the potential for assistance to contribute significantly to the changes they seek; they are not casual about the negative impacts they experience. They feel strongly that the cumulative negatives from aid are damaging and neither necessary nor inevitable. And, if international assistance were to change so that these negatives no longer happened, then—they claim—it would become both more helpful and less wasteful. Across all contexts, people agree that specific changes could enable international assistance to become a more effective contributor to progress in poor countries.

People conclude that without genuine engagement of both recipients and providers in changing the aid system as it now works, international assistance will continue to save some lives (greatly appreciated!); provide some useful infrastructure as well as much that is not useful or sustainable; benefit some people and marginalize others (often reinforcing preexisting social and economic inequalities); weaken local structures, and undermine local creativity; and simply waste a great deal of money and time contributed by both external and internal actors.

If this many people, at many levels in their societies and with varying degrees of involvement in international assistance efforts, in all the countries where we listened said these things—as they did—then it is important to hear them. The fact that they report these impacts and still urge us to keep providing assistance (but to do so in smarter ways) shows great faith in our ability to hear, and to change. They set forth both an opportunity and an obligation that all of us who are engaged in international assistance take on the challenge of changing some of the fundamental ways that aid is organized. Why this is important and how it can be done are the subjects of the remaining chapters of this book.

• • • • • • • • • •

CHAPTER FOUR

WHAT'S WRONG WITH THE CURRENT AID SYSTEM?

... in which we examine the prevailing delivery system approach to international assistance and explore how it shapes, and can distort, outcomes.

International Assistance as a Delivery System

In the eyes of people in countries that receive aid, international assistance is a multilayered and sometimes overbearing delivery system for resources and expertise from wealthier people and countries to poorer people and countries.

Is this a problem? And, if so, how and why?

A Brief History

The international assistance community had its origins in a generous response to suffering and need. In a world where innocent civilians were caught in wars, where some people faced drought and famine and lived their lives in extreme poverty, other people who lived with abundance organized, first private and then public, responses to address these needs. Both civil society groups and many governments initiated programs for war relief, disaster aid, refugee asylum and resettlement, and economic development. They raised funds and recruited staff to deliver succor and support to people suffering from disasters, conflict, and/or poverty.

As the media has increasingly brought the hardships of crises and poverty to the entire world's attention, the system for responding to such needs has grown in terms of both actors engaged in it and resources allocated to it. With years of experience and learning, it has developed into the complex enterprise of multilateral organizations, bilateral development aid agencies, international and local NGOs, community-based organizations, foundations, diplomats, banks, consultants, contractors, companies, academics, development "experts," and more.

During the more than half century of organized international assistance, many different approaches have emerged. Some have involved large, costly investment projects, while others focused on micro-credit and "small is beautiful" efforts. Some engaged at the community level, others at national and regional levels. Some emphasized private enterprise, others collective action; some, self-reliance and others, trade promotion. Some focused on sector-by-sector improvements, others urged integrated development; some saw the strengthening of government as central, while others pursued support to civil society as the way to bring desired socio-political change.

These varying and sometimes contradictory approaches to foster positive change grew out of learning from experience and, sometimes, from untested theories of change. On occasion, they have been prompted by failure. As it has evolved, the international assistance enterprise has come under increasing scrutiny and criticism. When the media shows images of people who have walked many miles to find food waiting at a feeding center where supplies are insufficient or delayed, aid agencies are accused of inefficiency. When an investigative reporter writes an article about a powerful person siphoning off aid to build his luxury mansion, the donor public is dismayed by the lack of accountability. National legislative bodies that allocate taxpayers' monies as well as individual investigators, politicians, and media have questioned the costs and benefits of international assistance. Some have even sought to abolish it. Pushed by these challenges, but also always by wanting to improve their own performance, aid providers have continually sought new approaches to improve the efficiency and effectiveness of international assistance.

Trends in the International Assistance Approach

Two broad trends dominate today's approach to international assistance. Both are motivated by the urge to improve outcomes.

From Response to Prevention

First, the international assistance system has taken steps to shift from response to prevention, from reacting to crises to solving problems proactively. The guiding language has changed from "charity" to "capacity building," from serving "victims" to supporting "survivors," from "war relief" to "conflict transformation," from "asylum" to "protection," from decrying ineffective governments to the promotion of "good governance." These changes are intended to improve the sustainability of progress made with international support by addressing the systemic problems that underlie needs and promoting "ownership" of aid efforts by aid recipients themselves.

The focus on prevention fits within the delivery mode of assistance. Aid providers deliver ideas, techniques, advice, and training—and, of course, material resources— to people whom they judge need help in solving the problems or addressing the fundamental weaknesses in their societies. They specify "deliverables" to raise funds and report on the progress. Aid agencies provide training to people in recipient communities to build the capacities that the aid-providing community deems are missing. The scheduling of the project cycle—indeed the packaging of assistance into projects or programs—reinforces the approach and the mindset of delivery by specifying the things aid agencies will provide to recipient communities in a given period.

Aid as a Business

The second prevalent trend in today's international assistance approach is the adoption of business principles and practices by many aid providers. This trend is based on a sense that improving the efficiency of aid's delivery will ipso facto also improve its effectiveness, and it is primarily motivated by the aid providers' desire to be more accountable both for funds spent and results achieved.

> 66 It is no longer humanitarian work; it is a business. This made me ask myself if I am working for the people or if I am working for the money. 99
>
> - Local NGO staff, Myanmar/Burma

It is not surprising that in a broad international pro-privatization climate, international aid providers looked to the private sector for tools and systems to improve the aid system's efficiency. Increasingly, aid donors and agencies have adopted the language of business. They talk about "value for money," "results-based management" and, as noted above, "deliverables." CEOs and boards of directors of aid agencies discuss their "return on investment" and the "branding" of their organization's work to distinguish it from others. With donor support, consortia of aid agencies have developed standards for "professionalism" in the aid industry. In addition, a number of international NGOs have recruited corporate representatives to their boards of directors or hired people from the private sector to lead their organizations.

"Many people view interventions as a money-making business, and the humanitarian as well as volunteer spirit that was the driving force has disappeared as most actors have become materialistic."
(Director of a local NGO, Kenya)

"The NGOs become service companies that make a profit from international aid." (An agronomist, Ecuador)

"They come into the camp to make profits for themselves."
(Leader in an IDP camp, Timor-Leste)

> **"The benefits are for them alone. They have salaries, we don't."**
> (Disaster survivor, Bolivia)
>
> **"NGOs are selling Indonesia by coming to villages, collecting data, and providing this data to donors in exchange for funding."**
> (Group of villagers in Indonesia)
>
> **"I believe that our black people are a big experiment in development, and that the information on this experiment is in Quito."**
> (Indigenous community leader, Ecuador)
>
> **"I think that Mali is becoming a laboratory to experiment with pedagogy and teaching. I ask myself, what are the donors' interests and why are they doing this? The tools come from the outside and are very often not adapted to the Malian reality."** (School teacher, Mali)
>
> **A woman in Bosnia-Herzegovina said that a number of NGOs had come to her area and, seeing her damaged house, taken her picture in front of it. However, none of these had ever come back to help her rebuild. She later heard from a friend of hers who had left Bosnia and gone to another European country that her picture with her damaged house had been put onto a fund-raising poster by one of the agencies that had taken her picture. It was being widely circulated in the country to which her friend had emigrated!** (Listening Project Report, Bosnia-Herzegovina)

Increasingly, contractors and even corporations have entered the international aid business. As profit-making entities, they recognize an opportunity to compete for donor government contracts, citing their strong management and delivery skills. In some countries hard hit by disasters or wars, where aid flows and public spending are increasing, the aid "industry" is the only one growing, creating opportunities seen by new actors in the aid system. Donor governments are also increasingly encouraging public-private partnerships.

Interestingly, and we cannot overemphasize this point, the adoption of business principles among aid providers has been markedly *selective*. For example, the international assistance community gives little attention to the fact that, even while aid providers seek to emulate business practices, many corporations recognize their own weaknesses in intercultural colleagueship and have turned to NGOs to learn how to relate better to the communities where they work. Even as aid tries to become more "business-like," private sector actors realize that they need to learn more about the principles of effective assistance.

Further, while corporations depend on the satisfaction of the end users of their products and services for survival, aid agencies depend on donors to whom they "sell" their projects and programs to provide aid to recipients. An aid agency does not need to receive the approval of aid recipients to continue to receive donor funding. This is demonstrated by the regularity with which aid providers dismiss recipient criticisms, saying that they "have heard all this before." A business entity could not survive in the face of this kind of repeated criticism from its clients.

The Delivery System Theory of Change

These two trends in international assistance—a shift from response to prevention and the adoption of business principles—embody and operationalize the theory of change that drives today's international assistance. This theory of change is:

> By efficiently providing tangible and intangible inputs, international actors can effectively cause, catalyze or support positive economic, social and political change in other countries.

The brief history of aid above traces the origins of this theory of change. Prompted in its early days by generosity and charity, those providing international assistance literally packaged up items collected in their better-off countries and delivered them to meet needs in countries where people suffered. As the aid system evolved, education, training, and advice were added to the provisions and the processes of delivery became more layered and complex. Still, the belief that the provision of inputs by external actors can prompt or support appropriate change in others' countries supports a delivery system theory of change.

The question is: Is this the right theory of change for international assistance? How does this theory influence the *system* of aid that, as we saw in the preceding chapter, produces what many people in recipient countries see as cumulative negative (intangible) impacts?

We turn now to explore what people in recipient societies say about aid as a delivery system. Their concerns focus on three areas: aid processes, aid providers, and aid purposes.

Effects on Aid's Processes

People describe five effects of the delivery system approach on the processes of assistance. They do this from experience and observation, not from theory, and they point to these tendencies as ones that can undermine aid's effectiveness.

1. A focus on delivery puts the focus on what is missing and needs to be supplied.

When an agency is expert in the delivery of certain goods or services, it tends to look for people who need them and for places that lack them. The starting point for its relationship with a society is, then, a focus on "needs assessment" rather than on existing strengths and capacities. However, meeting a need does not necessarily solve the problem that produces this need, and if help is provided without connecting to existing capacities, it can undermine them. Unless the problem is solved and existing capacities strengthened, the need may well rise again. For a business, this idea makes sense—repeat customers provide a steady revenue base. But for international aid agencies, a needs focus perpetuates dependency rather than supporting self-determination.

> 66 People come from the outside and do not spend time to get to know the community and the area. They see what is on the surface and they only see problems. 99
>
> - Spiritual leader, Thailand

2. A focus on delivery translates into supply-driven assistance where providers make decisions and choices even before they talk to receivers.

Preplanned and prepackaged projects are intended to improve efficiency. Businesses realize economies of scale when they distribute standard products in multiple markets. However, when aid suppliers make plans, without the involvement of people in the area where the activity is to occur, their assistance can ignore recipient priorities. They may deliver the wrong things at the wrong time or in the wrong way. Many recipients comment on how often this happens and how wasteful—and, therefore, inefficient—it is. If a business were to supply customers with unwanted products or services, it would find no market and would have to adapt its production or cease to exist. Yet, international assistance agencies can supply unwanted goods or services that they, as providers, determine to be "needed," without apparent penalty as long as they can sell the idea to their donors.

"It will just be a waste of a project ... because it is designed far away and brought out to people." (Ministry official, Timor-Leste)

"NGOs look at immediate needs, but may not be aware of why there's a problem. Why is the child sick? They need to stay longer to get an idea of the real problems." (Local resident of Kabul, Afghanistan)

"There are times that NGOs do not provide what people really need. For some NGOs, the projects come from above, top-down. They should listen to the people from the communities." (Community members, Myanmar/Burma)

"A local CBO funded through foreign donor funds has been surveying the surrounding communities in preparation for upcoming 'peace committees.' We have no idea what these are, and what they will do. We are not sure if this is something we need, we are just waiting to see what will come out of these surveys. I am baffled about how projects like this are decided on." (Woman in a village, Sri Lanka)

"Donors want to put communities into the same mold. Instead of adapting project activities to fit the funding, the funding should be adapted to meet our needs.... Donors should be tuned in to our needs and priorities. They should not impose. They should ask for input from the bottom, from the grassroots level. Projects that parachute from on high will not succeed." (Staff of a government rural development program, Mali)

"NGOs have an attitude that you have to do what we tell you. They act like this is a donation we should be grateful for. Like it is a relationship where they are powerful and we are not. They tell us what to do and how to do it or they threaten to cut off funding.... We are not stupid, we know they need us to make money.... There is not enough listening and understanding of local leadership skills and local coping skills. It feels like projects are becoming funder-driven."
(Long-time foreign aid worker, Thai-Burma border)

3. A focus on delivery brings a focus on growth and spending.

For a business, if delivering some is good, then delivering more is better. Donors, implementing agencies, and local partners also have come to equate success with growth. It is rare for governmental donor agencies to ask their legislative bodies to lower allocations for aid and, in turn, aid providers, including NGOs and private contractors, as well as their local partners, generally increase program requests year by year. NGOs continually try to expand their donor base and market share. Growth is taken as an indicator of effectiveness when, in fact, it may only be an indicator of spending capability.

Aid agency field directors say that they are promoted and respected if they "grow" their portfolios or budget every year and gain little recognition when they manage to save money for their agencies. Aid donors urge implementing agencies to monitor and maintain the "burn rate" of funds to keep on schedule. When aid budgets are under-spent, donors consider this practice "bad management" and often cut future funding. By contrast, in many businesses, cost savings can be rewarded by bonuses.

But, as noted, more people in recipient societies describe aid as "too much" rather than "not enough." They focus on the need to "stop waste" rather than "grow" assistance. The drive to deliver more aid, while greatly appreciated in some massive disaster or conflict situations, runs counter to recipient country goals of self-reliance and donor policies to promote local ownership and sustainability. Further, it provides opportunities for diversion and corruption.

4. A focus on delivery brings a focus on speed.

Many aid agencies (especially those engaged in humanitarian assistance) equate efficiency with "timeliness," and timeliness is regularly interpreted to mean speed. In development, peace-building, or human rights activities, programs are usually funded in one-, two-, or three-year cycles. In all types of programs, aid agencies submit proposals and write reports claiming achievement of grand goals on fixed and regular schedules in brief prescribed periods. Delays are frowned upon. Late submission of proposals disqualifies applicants; late submission of reports counts as poor management. While a business seeks rapid turnover of products, an aid agency seeks rapid turnover of projects.

Time pressures cause aid agencies to cut corners in terms of community consultations and to make assumptions about local circumstances. The pressure to deliver "development," "human rights," or "peace" in short project bursts is again seen by people on the recipient side to be wasteful and unrealistic.

> 66 Some NGOs are run like businesses. The donors are not helping us to be respectful because they come with their new ideas, trends and we have to jump.... We end up with ridiculous time frames to do things. We cut out the process and spend the rest of the year doing damage control. 99
>
> - Head of an INGO, Thai-Burma border

5. A focus on delivery means that monitoring and evaluation also focus on delivery.

An efficient business keeps its costs down. NGOs and their institutional and private donors mirror this practice by monitoring and emphasizing low overheads as a common measure of efficiency. Keeping overhead costs low relative to field program costs is taken to signal that an agency spends its money directly on helping people (considered the agency's outputs) rather than on headquarters salaries and offices (representing inputs).[3] Whether an agency delivers tangible goods or intangible services, its reporting on deliverables is often focused on cost per quantity delivered and whether the delivery was on time. Monitoring and evaluation processes focus on what has been done rather than on what has happened because of what was done. Although many aid providers are concerned to know impacts (and often are asked to report on them), in actuality, many say that they really do not track or report on the long-term and unexpected impacts or side-effects of their actions because these are hard to trace and are not required for renewal of funding.

"Donors are in a hurry to spend the money otherwise they won't get it next year—so this sets in motion a circle of requests." (Aid consultant, Solomon Islands)

"We all knew the good development principles like participation or conflict sensitivity, but in the rush of post-disaster relief, very few were able to uphold such principles because of requirements to spend money fast." (Director of a local NGO, Sri Lanka)

Some people said that many projects have been over-budgeted for no good reason. For example, a donor paid up to 1 million shillings for a toilet in one of the slum areas. A priest said this is happening because "Donors are always in a hurry to ensure that their money circulates and they care less about the impact being realized. It satisfied them to note that they funded a project and organizations A, B, and C. Our dream is that the money brought for the people is actually used for the people." (Listening Project Report, Kenya)

"What impact are you talking about? The impact is just spending money. Goods are delivered with no sense of social development. There is no interest to develop people; it's all reduced to practicality. Just know how to write a report. The focus is on skills put in the framework of outputs with no reflection included." (Director of a local NGO, Lebanon)

"Development isn't measured by the number of projects we receive or that are being implemented, but it should be measured on the strategy or the process of how to sustain a certain project." (Farmer, Philippines)

---

[3] The OECD-DAC Evaluation Criteria defines efficiency as "an economic term which is used to assess the extent to which aid uses the least costly resources possible to achieve the desired results." *OECD-DAC, DAC Criteria for Evaluating Development Assistance.* (Paris: OECD, 2000)

> "We need strategic, long-term partnerships with donors. The impact doesn't come overnight. We need to know that we can rely on their support not only tomorrow. If they want to make a change that lasts, they need to start taking longer breaths." (Coordinator of local NGO in Lebanon)

> "Donors only look at the ratio of expenditure to number of beneficiaries, so several of our proposals were not funded by donors. I suggest that donors should adjust selection criteria ... donor interests and needs of people do not always align.... Even if the number of people is small, they still need aid as they are very poor." (Secretary of a community council, Cambodia)

> "We have deliverables on a finished project, and we measure the end of the project. But there is no true monitoring, like an impact study that shows what the true impact is." (Teacher, Philippines)

> "Donors only monitor the money spent. They do not monitor the impact." (Ministry official, Cambodia)

Effects on Aid's Actors

The emphasis on delivery also has effects on the range of people involved in assistance efforts, according to many who observe delivery from the receiving side. They describe impacts on themselves as recipients, on the providers of assistance, and on the local organizations that become the "partners" of international aid agencies in the delivery of assistance.

1. When delivery is the focus, people in recipient societies become askers rather than doers.

Attitudes and actions of aid recipients are affected by a focus on delivery. To many, this is one of the most disturbing results of the delivery system. Even though most are clear that they do not want to need aid, they tell how—as aid recipients—they develop skills focused on getting the most aid they can, rather than on developing without assistance. Entrepreneurs become experts in proposal writing, not in running businesses; others become good at manipulating the system by appearing to meet the poverty or other criteria they know will "qualify" them for aid.

> " People's personal values change as a result of assistance. In the beginning, they helped each other and volunteered. In times of scarcity this is so, but when the money pours in, people become dishonest, greedy and even lack respect. "
>
> - Monk, Sri Lanka

Some point to societal distortions such as a loss of community sharing and volunteer spirit they had before aid arrived. Somehow, people say, the incentives of the delivery system business model evoke these perverse responses so that recipients, themselves, perpetuate their own dependency.

"The role of the NGO is just to bring what they have and dump it to us. We are grateful for what we have, but we are beggars. We can't choose and just take what we are given." (Food aid recipient, Zimbabwe)

"Donors require that we establish associations in order to be eligible for support, but these associations have in some cases become the source of our misfortune. It can happen this way. For example, I create an association and I am the president. My sister becomes the secretary and another sister becomes the treasurer, so it becomes a family affair. I can easily mobilize 100 other women to become members of my association, but they won't have the right to question things or have their say. When the funding arrives, you are marginalized if you keep asking questions. All the association's income goes to the president. When the donors return, the association's leaders convene some of the members and pay them to attend a donor's meeting. The donor is happy and concludes that all is going well. But, in fact, nothing is going well! The funding comes to those who know how to work the system." (Leader of a women's association, Mali)

"The 200 organizations, foundations, and agencies that have worked in the area represent a loss instead of a gain, as regards the lack of empowerment. The people become accustomed to requesting when they see this market of aid." (Parish priest, Ecuador)

"The bottom line of people coming in from outside is that they have to write a good report and account for all the money spent. They come with predetermined templates and formats that the local staff then have to follow, even at short-term notice." (Businessman, Solomon Islands)

In Bosnia, a number of people said that the donor procedures and laws on tendering required agencies to accept the cheapest offers/bids, but that often the quality was not good. This was a big problem in reconstruction projects, where one can now see paint peeling or uninhabitable buildings due to the use of sub-standard materials. (Listening Project Report, Bosnia-Herzegovina)

"Work in templates is easy; they are available. But to do it right you need more time and money and effort. Template projects get more visibility." (Student, Lebanon)

"The intermediary NGOs between the donors and the population are like traders. It is a very profitable business for them ... there is something that doesn't ring true with them. The results are not up to the level of the funds they have received." (Private businessman, Mali)

"Most donors only fund NGOs who are then expected to fund CBOs. This creates a lot of bottlenecks." (Farmer, Kenya)

"We are here to be partners but they treat us as construction workers. We have to finish the job on time, regardless of the problems. They care for the deadline and act like the commander." (Leader of a local NGO, Cambodia)

"International aid is like a large ice cube. As it gets passed through many hands, it becomes smaller. Some beneficiaries get only a few drops." (Town official, Sri Lanka)

2. Being in the business of delivering distorts the focus of donors and operational agencies.

Aid providers raise funds from both government donors and the public based on promises to deliver. Fundraising departments of aid agencies report that ads that emphasize people's needs and vulnerabilities excite more generosity than messages about supporting recipients' capacities.

The need to prove effectiveness in the marketplace of international assistance causes donors and operational agencies to focus on quantifiable results that can be documented, often in yearly (or more frequent) reporting cycles. Increasingly, donors demand—and agencies feel compelled to provide—reports on "value for money," basing their calculations on costs of delivery relative to how many people they help. The emphasis on efficient delivery thus permeates the attitudes and choices of donors and operational agencies as they seek to prove their value in quantifiable terms.

> " We now have the systems in place to deliver accountability to beneficiaries. "
>
> - Senior executive of an international NGO

3. In the delivery system approach, local partners are seen as and treated as "middlemen."

Much international assistance is channeled through local partners, a process intended to build local capacity and respect existing structures. However, many in recipient societies see these partnerships as barriers to effective work and siphons for funds that should be better used in direct support of communities. The long chain of assistance increases the distance between donors and recipients, costs money, provides opportunities for diversion of funds, and reduces international aid agency accountability.

The recipient society "partners," themselves, say that they are caught between donor demands and communities' priorities. They feel they have little power to shape assistance efforts when the system is organized to deliver goods, services, ideas, and models that originate from what providers have to offer.

> " The role of the 'donor' does not have to be a detached funding role. It can be a partnership. Unfortunately, international NGOs don't build capacity of national NGOs. Even when they work through local partners, the local NGO simply becomes a delivery mechanism, not a full partner. Partnership requires building relationships. That takes time. But most international NGOs have donors who demand fast and visible results. There is a disconnect in the way most agencies envision their missions and goals and the way they implement their projects seeking rapid outcomes. "
>
> - NGO leader, Thailand

Effects on Aid's Purposes

1. Competition Instead of Collaboration

International assistance efforts, especially in crises where a plethora of agencies respond to emergency needs, are criticized for duplication and redundancy. A business-oriented emphasis on efficiency would suggest that ineffective deliverers would be winnowed out, but the number of international and local NGOs and private companies in the aid business continues to grow.

> " Hunger has no flags, but we know very well that external aid, and more so the intermediaries of the resources of international cooperation, do have their flags, flags of all colors. "
>
> - Indigenous man, Ecuador

At the same time that both donors and recipients call for greater collaboration and coordination, the necessity for each aid agency to be seen as delivering more, and doing so more rapidly and efficiently than every other agency, in order to gain funding (market share) promotes competition. Logos on t-shirts, vehicles, and donated goods provide publicity that increases an agency's prominence, but not necessarily its effectiveness. Pressures to differentiate their work from that of other aid providers undermine joint analysis and operational collaboration.

"I believe ... that they want to give out things quickly and to work with the easily accessed community because of competition. They do not want to address the real needs, but to try to show how successful their aid delivery mission is." (Villager, Myanmar/Burma)

"NGOs are fighting for the same beneficiaries and the most affected people because it is better for their reports and for their donors. They don't talk to each other. Don't bring your conflicts and tensions here." (Buddhist monk, Thailand)

"There is only one time we saw staff of one of these international NGOs come and meet us—they came to unveil the sign about their funding here. We haven't seen anyone that belongs to that sign since then." (Local woman, Thailand)

People talk about competition between and among aid agencies at all levels. At the local level, where services are provided by different agencies, communities are often confused when different donors provide different types of assistance and services ... donors' different approaches and methodologies make work more difficult for the implementers ... [and] sometimes lead to suspicion of local NGOs or CBOs for not using the money properly, when in fact different donors have funded different things.... CBOs often do not work together, but rather compete with one another over resources and to survive. People suggested the combining efforts of different donors and implementing agencies could achieve more impact and reduce the competition and waste. At each level, it seems to people in communities that agencies are looking for the best deal, not necessarily what will help them achieve their objectives... At each level, it seems to community members that donors want to take credit for their own projects or groups, and the NGOs and CBOs involved along the way are seeking credibility and funding, rather than focusing on supporting real change in communities. However, if the projects fail, people said that no one seems to want to take the blame.
(Listening Project Report, Kenya)

"Many organizations are just interested in visibility. As soon as their logo is on the wall, they are satisfied. What is written in their brochures and newsletters is often not the reality." (Refugee, Lebanon)

"It would seem that those who act as intermediaries of international cooperation want us to remain poor; they help us in certain things, but at the same time, they keep us poor in others, in order to continue with the 'business of aid.'" (Afro-Ecuadorian man, Ecuador)

2. Concern with Survival Rather than Not Being Needed

Few international assistance agencies ever go out of business. The sizable, established, and interlocked aid enterprise has its own momentum or, as people in recipient societies often note, a vested interest in its own survival. Positioning the purpose of aid as meeting "needs" guarantees that aid agencies will always be "needed." Managers of the aid agencies recognize that they must keep income flowing by promising deliveries so they can maintain staff levels so they can be prepared to provide assistance again. Incentives for aid providers to work themselves out of a job—to support people so that they do not need external help (though not all needs may be met)—fade in relation to incentives to survive, grow, and continue to deliver.

Inherent Contradictions and Dilemmas

At base, the purpose of international assistance is to support people to develop their own economy, build their own peace, achieve good governance, and protect their own human rights. If the purpose of international assistance is to help people so that they no longer need assistance, then those providing assistance should be working to grow smaller—that is, working to go out of business.

Is the theory of change that supports the pursuit of effectiveness through efficient delivery of goods and services the right theory on which to base this enterprise? Many on both the recipient and donor sides of the enterprise would argue not. The evidence the Listening Project has gathered shows that, as is true of most theories of change, this theory is partly right and partly wrong.

This theory is right in that it does reflect the reality that people and countries with more resources (tangible and intangible) will and should be ready to offer support to people with fewer resources. This is what aid involves. The resource flow is from some and to others—and this flow is a form of delivery.

However, people on the receiving end (joined by many who provide assistance) observe inherent contradictions in the theory when it is operationalized in the current aid system.

Recipients report that the steps taken to increase efficiency and effectiveness in the *delivery* of assistance have increasingly located analyses, decisions, and choices at the delivery center. As the aid system has become more organized and coordinated at the top, people on the receiving end have seen their own voice curtailed. Many feel that the delivery system objectifies them. Some feel that international actors use their poverty to raise funds, and many say that more precise policies and standardized procedures among aid providers have reduced the space for them, as recipients, to be involved in considering options, weighing alternatives, and developing strategies for their own development.

> **"There is a disconnect between the needs of the people and what agencies are doing. Top-down is not a good relationship."**
> (University faculty member, Afghanistan)
>
> **Local NGO staff suggested that it is important not to come into a community offering goods but to spend significant time building a relationship.** (Listening Project Report, Cambodia)

Bolivians talked about the importance of a relationship of confidence, of NGO involvement and willingness to engage seriously, as well as the importance of good-faith interactions to help with impartiality, transparency and honesty. (Listening Project Report, Bolivia)

"We ask international agencies that come into our district to build capacity so that people can begin solving their problems on their own."
(Local government official, Zimbabwe)

Kenyan people in all regions of the country suggested that donors (which included INGOs) should visit and monitor their projects more frequently to maintain their relationships and to be sure the resources are being used appropriately. Many people felt that donors seem to just spend the money but then do not visit and verify the reports they get to see if the work is done, whether their standards are met, and if the projects are maintained. Donors have told them that "we don't want to be here to breathe down your back," but people want them to be present to show their concern, to understand their difficulties, and to ensure more relevant assistance. In the call for more presence there was a desire among people to share experiences with outsiders. They want donors and partners who can listen and also bring other ideas and programs for implementation. (Listening Project Report, Kenya)

People in recipient communities in every location said that, instead of being in the business of delivery, aid providers should be "present." Many ascribe great and positive changes to the single idea of presence, noting that if "donors spent time with us," they would "understand our realities," "provide appropriate things," "reduce corruption," and be able to develop respectful, trusting relationships. Listening Teams were struck by the universal and repeated call for aid providers to be "present."

Does this mean that people in recipient societies want international donor and aid agency staff to visit or live with them all the time? Clearly, the answer is no. Officials in government ministries certainly do not want even more delegations to visit; such visits, they say, already consume inordinate amounts of their time. And poor people in rural villages certainly do not want to host international visitors each day!

Presence, it became clear, is a short-hand way that people on the receiving side of international assistance express the great distance that they feel from aid providers.

International and local staff of assistance agencies (and their bosses!) frequently say that they "do not have time" to simply listen to and talk with people because their agencies expect them to focus on "project activities," programmed around delivering aid on time and on budget. The delivery system, reflecting some truth about the direction of resource flows, at the same time distances providers and recipients from each other in ways that, many people feel, reduce positive impacts.

The chapters that follow will trace the effects described here and explore how to imagine and develop alternatives to overcome the contradictions people observe between efficiently delivering things and developing problem-solving relationships.

• • • • • • • • • •

CHAPTER FIVE

DONOR POLICIES, DONOR AGENDAS

... in which we describe aid recipients' perspectives on the external interests and agendas that influence international aid, and the effects that these have on their societies.

People in recipient societies often talk with resentment about "donor policies" and "donor agendas." They feel that policies that serve donor interests are imposed from the top without regard for the impacts they can have within aid-recipient societies. These policies, people note, are tied to funding; if the policy is not followed, no funding is available. On this issue, most aid recipients do not distinguish among donors; they see multilateral and bilateral government aid providers and international NGOs that provide assistance as operating in very much the same ways. They see both as top-down decision-makers who apply their aid policies in different countries without sufficient recognition of the differences in these contexts.

From the Donors' Perspective

International assistance donors, on the other hand, see policies as one of their most important tools for shaping aid and ensuring its effectiveness. Policies are the medium through which donors articulate principles and priorities that provide the basis and rationale for what they do and how they do it. Policies set criteria for programming and funding decisions and procedures.

Government donors operate at two policy levels. As national entities spending taxpayers' money, they are expected to support and pursue the foreign policy, and increasingly the national security, agendas of their own governments. These policies may acknowledge that it is in the donor country's interest to encourage and support economic, social and political progress in aid recipient countries, but the foreign policy and other agendas that lie behind donor aid policies reflect primarily the donor government's concerns, regardless of how they affect recipient countries.

> " Of course aid is an instrument of foreign policy. Did you have any doubts about that? Following the political changes in 2005, a noticeable increase in donor interest and support to Lebanon has emerged. Prior to 2005, Lebanon was considered a "middle income country" and received limited amounts of grant financing. Following the 2006 war, Lebanon benefited from considerable grant financing that reflects the strong political support by donor countries to the current government. "
>
> - Consultant, Lebanon

At a second level, donor governments enact operational policies that set priorities for the values and principles their aid is intended to promote (such as democracy, gender equality, conflict sensitivity, human rights, and so on). Such policies have often emerged from previous experience and reflect the influence of interest groups within the donor countries. For example, in the 1960s and 1970s, international aid workers began to see that their efforts to help broad groups in recipient societies often inadvertently disadvantaged women relative to men. Simultaneously, the women's movement was spreading across all continents and countries as women, and men, recognized how societal patterns often perpetuate gender inequality. International assistance became one arena in which activists from both donor and recipient countries urged the formulation of aid policies to address women's equality as a value to be pursued through aid. Similar stories could be told of aid's growing policy emphasis on conflict sensitivity, human rights, good governance, etc.

The large international NGOs that have both public and private funds also adopt policies to shape their programs in accordance with their stated values, principles, and priorities. Many of these mirror those of their governmental donors. To the extent that such NGOs depend on government support, the broad policy framework governmental donor bodies set inevitably shapes their approaches. But NGOs also contribute to and help shape their government's policies so that these policies reflect NGO's values and concerns. As a result, the "policy context" for aid is largely set by international donors.

> " Some international NGOs come with their own agendas and are driven and influenced by the priorities set by their donors. "
>
> - Local person, Thailand

From the Recipients' Perspective

Many people in aid-recipient societies are well aware of both the political interests and the operational principles that donor policies reflect. They link donor policies to the general donor-driven delivery system, noting that donors deliver the policies that shape assistance in the same way that they, then, deliver assistance.

Nonetheless, with regard to donor governments' policy agendas, even when they disagree with them, people in recipient societies acknowledge the donors' right to pursue positions that serve their national interests. However, recipients describe situations in which the very intent of a donor's political policy is negated by its delivery in a given recipient context. Sometimes, they say, the core purpose of the policy is undermined. Sometimes, there are side effects that run counter to aid's purposes. And, too often, the results within the receiving country are problematic rather than supportive of the progress they seek.

In addition, many people in recipient societies agree with and share the values that underlie the donors' operational policies. They, too, want gender equity, peace, and human rights; they, too, want a strong civil society alongside an effective, responsible government. And, they want aid to come in ways that help achieve these goals. But, as with political agendas, they see flaws in policies that originate among donors and are delivered top-down. These, also, sometimes undermine the original policy intent and have counterproductive impacts.

> 66 In this region, there are over 100 NGOs that say they are working for the communities, but the aid is for those who come from the other side. This is a country that lives in peace. On the other side of the border, they live in war, but the lives of the people who live on the other side are much better than the lives of those of us who are on this side. I know the border well. That is why I ask myself why on the Colombian side, notwithstanding living in armed conflict, the rural communities have electricity, water, housing, and good schools, while on the Ecuadorian side, basic services do not exist and the few that do are in bad condition. It is ironic that many communities that do not have electricity have high voltage electricity lines passing right by in front of them. 99
>
> - Afro-Ecuadorian man in a border region, Ecuador

People on the receiving side of international assistance name three areas where donor policies, decided by those at the "top" and applied across all aid-receiving contexts, do not work. These are: 1) decisions about how to allocate assistance; 2) the lack of "fit" with local priorities; and 3) what appear to be frequent, and arbitrary, policy shifts.

1. Donor Policies: Who Gets Aid

People in recipient countries talk about how donors' political interests shape allocations of aid, both among and within countries. Some countries and some people receive little; others receive much. But, people say, the policy determination of who gets aid often ranks "need" secondary to donor country politics and agendas.

" Poppy politics, poppy policies. Nothing has worked, but why? The security collapse in Afghanistan has happened because we have not targeted the rural population. Seventy percent of the people are landless-farmers. The donors have pushed commercialization of agriculture. Who benefits from that? The landlords. In development plans, good governance is always one pillar. So why does bad governance continue? There's donor pressure, but they don't mean it. "

- Government employee, Afghanistan

In Cases of Political Isolation

When governments in donor countries isolate a regime because of its political ideology or practice (e.g., abuse of human rights), aid may be denied to otherwise needy people. Myanmar/Burma is a country where such donor choices, urged by human rights activists, prevailed for many years. In other cases, aid may be directed to show favor to particular countries, or groups within a country, who share a donor's political or national security interests.

International assistance to governments, whose politics are favored by donors, or withholding of support from disfavored regimes, can be a good thing. Few would argue with donor decisions that isolated the apartheid government in South Africa, and South Africans themselves urged this isolation. However, in many other places, people say that the impacts they experience from such outside agendas and policies are troubling.

For example, in Zimbabwe, people said they understood that international agencies gave only humanitarian assistance to avoid providing development support to Robert Mugabe's government. But, a grandmother who was caring for her orphaned grandchildren explained that a decision to provide aid only to people who tested positive for HIV/AIDS meant she got food to feed only one granddaughter, who was infected, while her other grandchildren were also hungry. She was amazed that donors set a political policy that forced her to choose among her hungry grandchildren. Others noted that the focus on humanitarian aid only for those affected by HIV/AIDs left able-bodied children and children who had living parents without any support. This neglect of healthy children and families was, they felt, shortsighted because it could undermine the country's future development. Others suggested that it is precisely when a government acts badly that its people most need the support of international agencies for survival and, even more, for support of programs that have potential to promote sustainable development.

In another example, national security policies of some donor countries have determined that Hezbollah should be isolated as a "terrorist organization." Within southern Lebanon, this designation means that the aid agencies of these countries avoid entire villages, who in turn often receive most of their humanitarian and development support from Hezbollah. Many in this area comment that this policy alienates these communities from the western donor countries and increases their loyalty to those that support rather than isolate them. Local NGOs also note that this kind of external political agenda can undermine their work, which, they say, is directed toward the same goals as those of the donors. Further, some describe how aid policies driven by an anti-terrorism agenda negatively affect trust and relationships among people in aid-recipient societies.

> " The donor came to visit us here in our office in order to offer funding for our program. But we directly rejected to work with their conditions. Politically I reject them. Morally I reject them. It is stupid to think that you can simply ignore the people you live with every day. We do not scan and judge our beneficiaries for their political and ideological attitudes. Yes, we have differences with many of these groups, strong differences even, and yes it is very difficult in many ways to find a common ground to work together. But we have to solve our differences in our own way, and this is not by isolating someone, on the contrary, by entering a dialogue with them. I do not accept this kind of interference. "
>
> - NGO staff member, Lebanon

To Encourage the Return of Refugees

Refugee returns have been promoted and supported for many years by donors who are committed to post-war reconstruction and reconciliation, and in some cases, multi-ethnicity. On the other hand, aid has sometimes been used to encourage refugees to return more quickly to homes they abandoned to get them to give up refuge or asylum in donor countries.

For example, in Bosnia-Herzegovina and in Kosovo, people talk about how the donor policies in support of "refugee returns" actually fed into and worsened inter-ethnic tensions rather than reducing them. People who had not left the area saw those who did flee getting aid to rebuild houses while they received little or nothing, and their resentment against these refugees increased. Some in Kosovo asked, "What do we have to do to get assistance—leave Kosovo and come back again?" The policy to support refugee returns thus increased intergroup tensions within the country, as well as some hostility toward donor countries rather than encouraging cooperation and peace as was intended.

"In the course of the war in 2006, international assistance came from the UN to be distributed to the people suffering from the war. However, the help could not go to 60% of villages in the south; it was forbidden because Hezbollah controls these villages. This is like you are blinding yourself! You alienate a portion of the community."
(Local NGO Director, Lebanon)

"INGOs provide assistance only to the places they can access. They don't come to the interior places and help IDPs."
(Women in a remote IDP camp, Sri Lanka)

"The Muslim community has been marginalized, even by the international community, especially after 9/11 and Osama bin Laden. Therefore, international assistance doesn't reach us and all we see are buildings of NGOs and some other people benefitting." (Muslim community members, Kenya)

"After the World Trade Center, the coup and terrorism, donor funding was cut by 60% and investors pulled out. Thus, there were less skilled jobs available and now only 10% of students can get jobs. Cambodia is short at least 100,000 jobs." (Village aid coordinator, Cambodia)

Aid to Myanmar/Burma is seen as politicized. Despite some international agencies having had a presence in the country for nearly 20 years, the amounts of international aid have been relatively small compared to other developing countries in the region. People noted that aid has increased greatly in three particular areas: 1) those affected by cyclone Nargis; 2) those where ethnically based militias agreed on a ceasefire with the government; and 3) those where the government has shut down opium production. (Listening Project Report, Myanmar/Burma)

"We got all this aid because the village was 'multiethnic.' The NGOs were fulfilling their own conditions. To get aid, not only does your community have to have many ethnic groups, they have to have problems with each other too!" (A group of shop owners, Kosovo)

To Address Conflict

> "It appears there is a need to be in a war situation before we can get assistance. We have to risk our lives in order to get development aid."
> - Community members, Philippines

In addition, in many war-torn areas, people tell how donor policies to help those who suffer from war mean that the communities who manage to maintain peace are overlooked and penalized. The sense that violence is rewarded because donor policies put priority on areas affected by conflict was echoed in Bosnia-Herzegovina, Kosovo, Lebanon, Philippines, Afghanistan, Solomon Islands, and elsewhere. In some cases, people say this focus creates perverse incentives for those seeking assistance.

For example, in Afghanistan, many people note that relatively secure provinces receive much less aid than those where there is open conflict. Some suggest that international assistance does not come to areas that have "neither Taliban nor poppies." A member of the Afghan Independent Human Rights Commission explained: "The government strategy vis-à-vis Bamiyan is problematic: priority goes to insecure areas. Some people are promoting insecurity in order to attract assistance. Many people say this." A field worker of an NGO echoed this concern saying, "If the child is not crying, the mother will not provide milk. The cry is the rockets. If we don't receive aid, we will have to make noise."

A Note on Media Influence

People in recipient societies note the influence of the media in affecting and shaping some donor priorities. By covering some conflicts, disasters, and other crises, they bring attention and resources to bear. However, places affected by chronic poverty or long-term conflict often get little or no coverage and, as a result, aid allocations can bypass areas where longer-term and sustained attention could help people make systemic progress. Again, people describe how aid allocations are responsive to pressures within donor countries more than to realities in receiving countries. For example, people in an area of western Kenya where there are recurring tribal clashes over land that do not get international attention, said, "If we could get media coverage, we could get more help."

2. Donor Policies: Mismatch with Local Priorities

The second issue of concern to many people with regard to donor policies is what they see as the misfit between external and internal priorities. As noted, the problem is not that people reject the values that drive the external policies. Rather, the problem is the external imposition of a policy priority that cannot be adapted through discussion to fit with and reinforce local priorities.

For example, while rebuilding houses in Bosnia-Herzegovina was a priority of donor countries pursuing policies of multi-ethnicity and refugee returns, people who had remained in the country during the war say that their priority was on rebuilding and restarting the economy. Similarly, in Kosovo, people note that the donor policy of encouraging reconciliation among ethnic groups could never succeed until their priority of determining their region's final status *vis a vis* Serbia was resolved.

> 66 If you ask me what my priority needs are and I tell you, but then you bring me other things instead, I will take them, but you did not help me. 99
>
> - Farmer near Timbuktu, Mali

In the eyes of many people in recipient communities, donors decide policy priorities and pursue their agendas in recipient countries without consultation, adaptation, or negotiation that aid recipients can participate in or influence. To be sure, many high-level international meetings are held where donor and recipient country leaders attend and where both sign and issue joint statements. A growing trend among the leadership of recipient societies is to assert their agendas and set terms for their interactions with aid providers.[4] The evidence from the field, however, indicates that even though donors have adopted policies to integrate aid efforts with recipient country planning, the policies have not been consistently translated into changed donor behaviors.[5] From the field, donor policies still appear to be top-down impositions of their priorities backed up by funding that is available only if the agenda or the policy is followed.

"If someone comes here and wants to do something, we don't say no because we don't want to say no to donors. There is a disconnect between the Poverty Reduction Strategy Papers (PRSPs) and other documents and what donors fund. No one reads or refers to them. Donors go where they want, not where they are needed, especially in projects channeled through the government." (District government official, Kenya)

"The projects depend on international and national politics but not on the community. For example, credit for cocoa, bananas, shrimp: giving money on top of money. What about the small producer?"
(Officer of a Provincial Council, Ecuador)

---

[4] Such as the Busan Partnership for Effective Development Cooperation signed at the 4th High Level Forum on Aid Effectiveness in late 2011.
[5] See, for example, the *2011 Survey on Monitoring the Paris Declaration* (Paris: OECD, 2011).

"Donors do a lot of assessments and focus groups, but then when what comes out of these focus groups doesn't fit their agenda, they simply change it to make it fit." (Lebanese researcher, Lebanon)

"There are policies of donor governments that the ministries are against, but they can't do anything." (Government employee in Kabul, Afghanistan)

"The donor agency never asked us what we actually needed or wanted, and the community did not want to refuse a generous offer even if we could not use it now. We hoped that one day, there would be a doctor sent to the community and then the [new but closed] health center could open." (Young man, Kosovo)

Some of the goals arise from external visions: improving living conditions, fulfilling the Millennium Development Goals, combating poverty, democratization, building of self-sufficiency, etc. Local visions are often less utopian and more practical because they confront the "how" of a complex situation. They focus on the immediate—for example, proposing only sources of employment. (Listening Project Report, Ecuador)

3. Donor Policies: Shifting and Changing Priorities

The perception that donor agendas are imposed from the top-down and override recipient priorities is exacerbated by the third donor policy problem identified by people in recipient communities—namely, the frequent shifts in priorities and changing donor "fads." People say that changes in donor priorities affect their efforts to make real and sustained progress. The freedom and frequency with which donors introduce new policies and shift funding allocations to pursue new agendas is, recipients say, disruptive and counterproductive in a number of ways.

66 People come in with different priorities and agendas. Objectives and frameworks change, and there is no consistency, so they don't learn from past mistakes. In civil society, development partners and the public sector, changes are politically motivated with ideological leanings, including appointments. Different people have different passions, and the transitions are never smooth. 99

- University lecturer, Kenya

Shifting Agendas Undermine Sustainability

Noting that their problems require long-term strategies, people in many countries at many levels say that donors' shifting agendas undermine the kind of programming consistency that is important to achieve sustainable results. They seek external engagement and funding support that they can rely on for long enough to achieve planned results. As agendas change and funding allocations shift to new priorities, aid recipients' own efforts can be undermined or abruptly stopped.

> **Many people talked about the problem of "project fashion" and the "trendiness" of donor funding priorities, which they felt were changing almost every year—from a focus on human rights, to the reconstruction of houses, to microcredit, to civil society, to peace building, etc. To many people, it seems as though there was no strategic plan for reconstruction and development and that there is a lack of continuity and long-term commitment to projects. One person noted, "It is hard to make peace between the donors' wishes and the real needs of the local community."** (Listening Project Report, Bosnia-Herzegovina)
>
> **The development styles of international cooperation generally respond to fads and schemes that are cyclical in fashion on a global level. The tendency of these fashions is to mimic globalization, generally not considering the particularities of each country.** (Listening Project Report, Ecuador)
>
> **"The weakness of donors is to sit somewhere and read reports. Quite often, donors assume they know every problem and can therefore prescribe solutions. They fail to consider the socio-economic and political realities on the ground. It is becoming clear that donors are obsessed with 'sexy' projects and change immediately when another 'sexy' issue comes up."** (University Lecturer, Kenya)

Shifting Agendas Undermine Local Control

Recipients say that changing donor agendas (and the misfit of external and internal priorities) also undermine local initiative and control of activities. If funding is tied to donor priorities and if these often shift in new directions, people on the recipient side feel they cannot take the lead in planning and implementing activities. They become passive recipients rather than active agents. Community members, CBOs, and local NGOs describe how they make projects fit into categories that they think can get donor funding based on the current donor agendas instead of promoting their own goals and strategies. Both local agencies and people in communities talk about how even though their interests and priorities do not match with those of donors' shifting agendas, they nonetheless often take whatever assistance is offered in hopes that it might help in some way. Some also say that they accept whatever is given because they do not want to say no to donors who might later provide something that will help or later support their priorities.

Shifting Donor Agendas Catch Implementers in the Middle

Shifts in donor funding priorities pose problems for international and local organizations that are engaged with local people and trying to support recipient priorities. These agencies say they feel caught between the local communities' visions and plans and the donors' agendas and priorities over which they have little control. Partnerships are weakened; they become only a delivery system for ensuring the speedy and efficient flow of funds. This affects immediate programming directions and relationships with the local communities. Time and effort are spent on managing expectations and tensions that could be better spent jointly addressing real problems. Suspicions of each others' motives and agendas increase, undermining the very idea of "development cooperation."

> " The [people in the] target groups don't care for the targets of the donors or the international politics. They want to see their situations improved. The NGOs or the implementing organizations are in between the two, managing the expectations of both sides. The expectations of our target groups may differ from those who give us money. We just have to admit that there may be a gap. "
> - International funder and implementer, Timor-Leste

Many local organizations describe how they adapt to changing donor agendas because they are dependent on foreign aid. In Cambodia, for example, a local NGO director said that his agency changes its mission every five years in order to keep getting donor funding. But another NGO leader said, "Donors shouldn't change their minds frequently. Education is not an area where the impact can be felt in just three years of support." Others noted that for persons living with HIV/AIDS, donor consistency was a matter of life and death.

"The pervasive attitude is that beggars can't be choosers. In many cases, we don't have much say in what gets funded. These programs usually benefit the donors in meeting their funding priorities. What we suggest often doesn't fit their menu of options. After much back and forth, we end up asking them, 'What do you want to fund?' And then we adjust. But we have also turned down funding because it hasn't met our priorities." (City official, Philippines)

"Some INGOs and donors have very little understanding of the priorities of the communities in which they work. Our local program priorities have to fall under the priorities and funding restrictions of the donor. We are restricted by their mandates which are 'peacebuilding' and 'civil politics, democratic leadership and governance.' Our objectives collide somewhere with these rigid sets of goals of outside donors. While trying to match our goals with your goals, we feel that we are constantly compromising on our original objectives and trying to find the best fit for our goals under your rubrics. For example, we are committed to build community leadership on the tea estates, but in our own way. In order to get the needed resources, we fit our particular vision under your funding priorities that only partially touch on leadership development."
(Leader of a community based organization, Sri Lanka)

People felt that the focus of external agencies varies and changes significantly, and that what is fashionable today is no longer so tomorrow. Sometimes the result seems not only confusing, but also, even illogical and unfair. Each external entity has its own policies, and they only rarely agree with other entities' policies. The people in communities—following the development methods in effect at the time and being careful not to offend those who have the power—often run the risk of letting themselves be guided in any direction. Sometimes the goals are not well-defined and the community, unaware, becomes an instrument of external agendas. (Listening Project Report, Ecuador)

"The local community expects that you are there to solve their problems; they don't know about donor agendas. Donors come with their agenda. Local organizations design their projects to fit the criteria, but it might not be what is most needed. When they come with their agenda, we think: Why do a needs assessment if the agenda is already decided?"
(Palestinian NGO staff, Lebanon)

What Does It All Add Up To?

Of course, donors develop policies to clarify their values and priorities, and establish criteria and standards for the support they provide. Aid-recipient countries recognize this and accept that donors operate in political environments that shape their policies and, hence, their priorities. At the community level, many people also share the majority of values that drive donor agendas and welcome international engagement around such issues.

They point out, however, that when donor policies and agendas undermine the values that they mean to promote, this is inefficient. They say that just because aid is political does not excuse it from being effective. They argue that actions must match words if policies are to promote effective programs for economic development, peace, good governance, and human rights. International donors themselves recognize that their policies can flounder in implementation. Many speak of the policy-program gap and seek ways to overcome it (sometimes by writing new policy documents!).

The commentary of people in recipient communities points to the location of policy initiatives as a problem. The way that donors develop policies reinforces the delivery system of assistance. The fact that donors largely discuss and write policies, which are seen as entirely top-down, undermines recipient country ownership of these policies and recipient community ownership of the programs developed in pursuit of the policies. This top-down approach undermines partnership and a sense of mutual respect. And it creates resentment. In addition, recipients see external agendas as overly prescriptive and, therefore, not easily adaptable to contextual variations and realities.

The Exceptional Case

As noted in previous chapters, an exception to the general resentment of the imposition of external agendas can be found in a widespread appreciation among recipient societies for the international promotion of gender equity. Although the attention to women's roles evoked considerable resistance in both donor and recipient countries when it first appeared, and appreciation for women's programming is not (yet) universal, this is an area where recipient countries have joined donor countries in both enacting policies and implementing strategies to make gender equity a priority. How this happened may provide clues about the development of policies that integrate external and internal priorities. Historically, women in recipient countries were as active and as visible in their advocacy of equality as women in donor countries. The thrust for the gender policies that donors adopted came from a broad, worldwide coalition of women and men who recognized the opportunity for international assistance to support a cause. It was a cause that was embraced even before policies were enacted by significant actors in all countries.

Donor conferences and donor and recipient country meetings, the adoption of a UN Decade for Women that kept the focus on this issue over an extended period (with funding to accompany the focus), and the engagement of numerous civil society organizations in programs to promote gender awareness and women's rights (also many—though by no means all—with donor support) help explain why results from pursuing this agenda may be seen as positive. Closer examination of the sequencing of events surrounding the adoption of a gender policy and tools for programming in this area may provide more useful lessons for closing the gap between policies and programs in other areas.

Conclusion

The learning in this chapter is not surprising, but it is critical. The lesson is that context matters. Policies applied in different contexts often have unintended negative impacts and can perversely cause people to seek to show they meet the criteria that the policies target.

Policies set at the international level with good intent have cascading effects that are often troubling in the contexts where they are applied. It may be right to isolate an oppressive leader, but this should not make a grandmother choose which grandchild to feed. It may be right to encourage multi-ethnicity in today's world, but it is not right to penalize people who remain in a war zone rather than flee. Reinforcing existing governance structures is good if they are just, but it runs counter to international assistance goals to reinforce oppressive wealth and power structures. A peacebuilding or stabilization policy should not, when applied, reward people who have fought and penalize those who have not.

People in aid-recipient societies, from national government officials to local community members, want the opportunity to talk about the various agendas, priorities, and policies that drive international action in their countries. They want to work with donors, and those who implement donor policies, to understand and integrate internal and external agendas. They want to explore common values and jointly design policies that embody these values. They want to work together to tailor broad agendas to local contexts to ensure that the impacts are consistent with the policy rather than contradictory to it. This is a reasonable and reachable goal.

● ● ● ● ● ● ● ● ●

CHAPTER SIX

THE PROCEDURALIZATION OF INTERNATIONAL ASSISTANCE: A DISTORTING INFLUENCE

... in which we explore how procedures intended to make aid more transparent and consistent become complicated, rigid, and counterproductive, reducing efficiency and effectiveness and wasting both time and money.

Standardizing Procedures: The Rationale in Brief

Organizations adopt procedures for good reasons. Procedures streamline and simplify recurring aspects of work. They support standards of consistency, predictability, and professionalism across programs and contexts. They reinforce transparency and fairness by clarifying the rules for all actors. They facilitate orientation of new staff and partners to institutional standards.

International assistance organizations are no exception. Individually and collectively, aid donors and aid agencies have developed standardized processes to translate their policies into efficient and effective field practice. Many have enacted internal management procedures, fiscal procedures, assessment procedures, procurement procedures, and beneficiary selection procedures, among others. There are monitoring and evaluation procedures and even procedures for evaluating the effectiveness of organizational procedures![6]

People in aid-recipient societies also value the predictability and clarity that these agency procedures are intended to provide. They, too, want to have standards and rules of behavior that they can rely on and work with, and to which they can hold agencies accountable.

In the context of international assistance, procedures are important for ensuring that the institution and its entire staff remain committed to the organization's priorities and accountable for the fundamental principles that underlie "best

---

[6] See, for example, DFID's *Essential Guide to Rules and Tools* for one such collection of procedures governing interactions with recipients of their grants.

practice." These principles, agreed to by most aid providers and aid recipients, include participation of local actors in all phases of project design, implementation, and evaluation; promotion of local ownership; sustainability of results; equitable distribution of benefits; and mutual accountability.[7] Many also point to the importance of contextual knowledge in pursuing these principles. Without common procedures, programming decisions can be ad hoc, optional, unpredictable, subject to manipulation, and dependent on individual improvisation, which can vary widely based on experience, proclivity, and knowledge.

Since everyone agrees on the principles that undergird good assistance and everyone agrees that procedures are needed to ensure commitment to these principles, one would expect that good procedures should lead to better results. Some have done so, serving both providers and receivers of assistance well by increasing transparency and fairness in the delivery of aid. However, repeatedly and across all contexts, people on both giving and receiving sides describe a downside to the growing numbers and complexity of international assistance procedures.

The Downside: Proceduralization

Providers and recipients of assistance describe procedures that "take too much time" and are "inflexible," "too complicated," or "counterproductive." Many talk about the ways that "tick-the-box" processes become so dominant that aid organizations and workers lose sight of the very values that these processes were intended to support. They also obscure contextual differences and limit adaptations to changing circumstances. Providers and recipients frequently describe how rigid templates for planning and evaluation obstruct creativity and innovation, and lead, instead, to pre-packaged and irrelevant or unwelcome projects.

> ❝ We all know that in order to reach the external aid resources, management and administrative procedures are required and we poor people don't have the time for carrying out so many procedures. ❞
>
> - Afro-Ecuadorian neighborhood leader, Ecuador

When donors or aid agencies assume that efficiency (presumed to be embedded in procedures) inevitably leads to effectiveness, they confuse compliance with systems for achievement of results. They focus their monitoring and evaluation attention on whether the boxes have been ticked rather than on whether the intended

---

[7] The Good Humanitarian Donorship Initiative, which produced a set of principles signed by a large group of donors in Stockholm in 2003, represents one comprehensive step in enunciating and codifying principles and good practice for humanitarian donors. Some of the principles for effective humanitarian donorship are now widely accepted in all other areas of international assistance, such as the Paris Declaration on Aid Effectiveness signed in 2005. The international NGO community has also developed corollaries in codes of conduct, the Istanbul Principles for CSO Development Effectiveness, an INGO Charter, and, in the form of partnerships, for example, has set standards for humanitarian work (SPHERE) and accountability (HAP).

outcomes and impacts have been achieved. Aid providers and recipients describe how procedures can, and do, sometimes undermine efficiency rooted in simple and clear practice. In short, they describe how processes and methods meant to improve impacts have become so "proceduralized" that they are counterproductive.

We have coined this quite awful word "proceduralization" (which we promise not to overuse!) to describe the codification of approaches that are meant to accomplish positive outcomes into mechanical checklists and templates that not only fail to achieve their intent but actually lead to even worse outcomes. The word is meant to resonate with "bureaucratization," which describes the process by which bureaucracies that are developed to accomplish large tasks become rigid and unresponsive to human concerns and the people who work in them become "bureaucrats"—often used as a pejorative term—who impede rather than facilitate accomplishment of the original task or mission.[8]

When relationships between aid providers and recipients are subsumed by standardized procedures that close off spontaneous and respectful interaction, then we can say that these relationships have become "proceduralized," and the values that the procedures were intended to enable are lost.

> 66 Donors demand task-focused work. Staff would love to have more time to talk to people in the camp, to spend the night in the camp. But, we have reports due, with facts and numbers and it needs to be right to keep the funding coming. 99
> - Long-time foreign aid worker, Thai-Burma border

The learning in this chapter comes from the people in recipient societies *and* from the reflections of people involved in providing aid. Both have an interest in ensuring the regular pursuit of the principles of good practice, and both see how many of the processes currently used to do so have become proceduralized. All want to see this corrected. Below, we describe how the principles of good practice are pursued through procedures and how these very often play out in the experiences of aid recipients and providers.

1. Principles of Participation, Ownership, and Sustainability

The three principles of participation, ownership, and sustainability are interlinked cornerstones of good practice and effective development, or peacebuilding. Some also argue that these same principles apply in humanitarian assistance because when recipients of emergency aid are involved in decisions about what they need and how it should best be provided—that is when humanitarian assistance is based on and supports people's own capacities of response—it also can feed into and support sustainable development processes. Insiders (people in recipient societies) and outsiders (external aid providers) all observe that when people participate

---

[8] Dare we also coin the word "proceducrats"?

in all phases of an aid effort, from conception of the idea, to the design and planning, to implementation, and through final evaluation, they will "own" the process and therefore be more likely to maintain the results. Participation leads to ownership leads to sustainability. Most people at all levels of the aid apparatus agree to this linkage.

" People are either dependent on aid or they are engaged with it—they are participating. If people are not involved with the project, they will not own it and take care of it. If the people are invested in the development, they will take care of that development. "

- A local NGO staff person, Cambodia

The linkage of these three principles—participation, ownership, and sustainability—is confirmed by positive and negative experience. That is, when people are thoroughly involved in planning and executing a project, they do own it and manage it for the long term. And, when they are not sufficiently involved, the reverse is true—little or no ownership exists and short-lived benefits result.

Even though the international assistance community has developed procedures to encourage the participation of recipients in planning and implementing projects, the vast majority of people in recipient societies report that they do not feel included in the critical decisions about assistance they receive. In their experience, many of these decisions have been made before an aid agency arrives in their area and there are few, if any, opportunities to add their ideas as the effort unfolds.

In several Ethiopian pastoralist communities, people said they were very engaged in the selection process and nomination of community members for skills training and that the participatory methods used by the NGO were appropriate and fair. Some recalled participating in meetings with experts or government people who came to talk to them. They saw some of their input later reflected in the projects and talked about open monthly meetings where they shared experiences and identified and prioritized problems. An NGO in this area supported these public meetings in an effort to revive the traditional system and increase transparency. [But in other areas] Some government officials said that international NGO projects are too donor-driven and that agencies rarely hold discussions with local governments on their budgets and long-term expectations. (Listening Project Report, Ethiopia)

People in Kosovo offered examples of effective three-way communication and partnerships between communities, a municipality, and NGOs in which the community worked together with the NGO to prioritize projects and carry out implementation. The community and municipality also played an active role in the selection of contractors, and all stakeholders within the community were expected to contribute to the cost of implementation, be it with financial support or in-kind support. One person commented, "Our participation was very valuable—we wanted to own it. Even if we did not always have the material support, we gave the moral support. That was always, always there." (Listening Project Report, Kosovo)

"This is how the verb 'to participate' is conjugated: I participate. You participate. They decide."
(An indigenous businessman and grassroots development worker, Ecuador)

"Everything is decided before you start the project. Some donors come to us with ready-made objectives so we have to channel them into our objectives. Once you get funded as a local NGO, you are strangled by the conditions you imposed on yourself in the proposal."
(Local NGO staff, Lebanon)

In Burma, there was a widespread feeling that, because communities were not adequately involved in the early stages, they did not know what to expect of aid agencies and did not view the aid they brought as belonging to themselves ... A project may be implemented in order to suit the needs of the organization, be it the need to implement a certain number or a specific type of project, regardless of whether that project will actually address a community need, or the need to disburse remaining funds before the end of a funding period. (Listening Project Report, Myanmar/Burma)

In Bolivia, people commented on the importance of NGOs engaging with them in a participatory fashion, which encouraged and allowed people's involvement in priority setting, project design, decision-making and management of participants, materials, and even funds. People also voiced disappointment, frustration, and even humiliation when NGOs refused to treat them in this manner and opted for a more vertical, authoritarian, top-down approach. (Listening Project Report, Bolivia)

Proposal and Funding Procedures

Aid providers and people in recipient societies name international assistance funding procedures as the starting point of limited participation. Aid agencies need resources to do their work, so they appeal to donors. Donors need assurance that aid agencies have well-thought-through plans worthy of their funding. They need to know who will be helped, how, and with what inputs. They need specificity about expected results; they want to know how the agencies will report these results, often in the language of "benchmarks" or "indicators" of success included in their logframe analysis.

To get funding, proposal-writing agencies therefore make some essential decisions before they can even put staff on the ground. Recipients say that donors and agencies talk about participatory development but do not provide time or financial resources to allow it. They ask why they see no procedures (and funding for them) for engaging recipients before proposals are submitted and funding allocations are decided. Further, because funding depends on proposals with a logical framework, conceived and elaborated by aid agency staff who, then, must submit donor reports demonstrating that their plan was "right," little space remains for people on the receiving side to insert their analyses.

> 66 INGOs have good techniques but are weak in mobilizing the community people since they have limited time-frame. Not all people from community know well about the organization and its purpose, and when the field staff cannot explain well to them, misunderstanding occurred. Since they cannot build the capacity of the community people, the projects are not sustainable. 99
>
> - Local man, Myanmar/Burma

Pre-packaged projects that arrive already designed and funded through proposal and funding procedures negate meaningful participation of recipients. Some people also point out that because proposal writing is a complicated procedure that takes skills they do not have, they must rely on others to do their proposals for them, and this further impedes broad involvement. In their experience, the procedures for proposing and getting funding for activities used by most aid agencies do not really encourage, or even allow, genuine participation.

Assessment Procedures

Household surveys, focus groups, questionnaires, and community meetings are procedures that aid providers use to identify needs, learn about local conditions, invite ideas, and engage people in considering options for programs. These tools should encourage participation, and hence, ownership and sustainability.

However, many people find that these procedures function as straightjackets. Where they are intended to gather data on existing conditions, they do so in predetermined templates which categorize people based on family size, wealth, needs, etc., for ease of analysis. When they are intended to invite ideas, they are focused on whether people want what is being offered, or not, rather than on hearing people discuss their priorities and suggestions for making progress. People feel as if their thoughts are supposed to "fit" into predetermined categories or options. And on the occasions when people say they are actually involved in an assessment, they find that procedures for using the information and the ideas they provide are nonexistent or inadequate.

> 66 Working in templates is easy. They are available. But to do it right, you need more time and money and effort. Template projects get more visibility. Some donors come with 'results-based frameworks' with all their definitions. This is meant to be a tool for better projects, but they spend half the year explaining what it is. 99
>
> - A Lebanese PhD student and consultant, Lebanon

Community Consultation

International aid agency staff often begin their work in an area by calling a community meeting to describe their plans. They also use these meetings to ask people for ideas and suggestions. This procedure should, of course, lead to involvement and ownership.

People in recipient communities say that this kind of consultation is excellent but more so in concept than in execution. They find that the styles of interaction of some international agencies limit recipients' participation. For example, people say that aid agency staff are always in a hurry. But in their cultures, discussions and decision-making take time; when staff call a meeting for a specific time when decisions are to be made, the process feels imposed and unnatural to them. Some recipients describe how within their own culture, people express disagreement in quiet ways that outsiders often do not recognize. They say that their sense of courtesy means they sometimes accept the ideas of outsiders out of politeness rather than because they really agree with them. Finally, people describe how some external aid providers are domineering or rude so that people in recipient societies simply shut down rather than engage. Many procedures of aid providers, people feel, are not attuned to cultural differences and leave little space for building relationships not focused on "getting the job done" and "meeting deadlines."

66 Foreign staff efforts are undermining Cambodian efforts to participate in a meaningful way. We have to spend time investing in the staff. INGO staff speak fast English and use big words, and by doing so, shut local staff out of decision making. Outsiders run the show; local staff are not even invited to management meetings. The NGOs and the donors have expectations that if you are empowered, you will speak out and stand up for your rights—basically be like the foreigner. Yet Cambodians are constantly communicating their wants and likes in ways that they feel is direct, but foreigners don't get this and expect more direct communication. 99

- International aid worker, Cambodia

So, the principles of participation, ownership, and sustainability are undermined by procedures for proposal writing to gain funding, assessment procedures that collect information in predetermined (externally designed) categories, and flawed use of appropriate tools when agency staff invite input from recipients without really listening to it. People see these tools, these procedures, as methods aid agencies employ only to justify predetermined decisions and then to claim to have been "participatory."

People in Mali regretted the fact that visits were very brief and that donors always seemed to be in a hurry. In their view, donors seem to be responding more to the needs of their own organizations and were more preoccupied with feeding their own systems (with reports, data collection, meetings, etc.) than observing, addressing, and learning from issues in the field. Donor representatives themselves lamented the fact that they have little time to go to the field to see activities first-hand and to meet with partners and beneficiaries. Time constraints and the additional costs that more frequent monitoring visits would entail were cited as reasons for the limited follow up on the ground. (Listening Project Report, Mali)

"The lack of flexibility and short time spans for projects—12 months—creates difficult conditions. Short time approaches are one of the main factors that instigate failure. In spite of this, the donors still ask for sustainability!" (Government official, Afghanistan)

The evidence from all our conversations suggests that most recipient communities are not being sufficiently engaged in aid programming and decision-making. There are common complaints that NGOs take a blanket approach and arrive with pre-planned programs, without doing appropriate needs assessment or consulting with the communities about their priorities. (Listening Project Report, Zimbabwe)

To many people in Kenya, international assistance was seen as a series of disjointed, one-off efforts to meet isolated needs, provided in ways that left incomplete, unsustainable results, rather than holistic interventions that made a long-term impact ... Many people talked about how the short-term nature of many aid projects, including the short reporting time frames in which they are expected to show impact, was a major challenge to making projects sustainable. They noticed that the emphasis on speed leads to cut corners and poor quality work. Short time frames and tight reporting deadlines and requirements also result in less time spent with communities doing the time-consuming consultations needed for sustainable outcomes. The funds come in installments that are deliberately small, thus the organizations cannot plan long-term for these funds. (Listening Project Report, Kenya)

Some people said that they had participated in many assessments and projects but that they had never seen any of the reports that had been written by international agencies or donors. A few did not have much hope of changing the system and one person said, "Why should we tell you what we suggest? No one ever listens to us. Even if you will listen, they won't, so why should we bother?" (Listening Project Report, Ethiopia)

Another issue relating to information and communication had to do with the various groups or intermediaries that visited communities to complete surveys and questionnaires, to conduct needs assessments or to carry out evaluations but provided little or no follow up afterwards. People felt a bit "used." (Listening Project Report, Mali)

An Additional Note on Sustainability: "Projectitis"

The international community largely relies on the project mode of delivery. This is true even in sector-based programming because what many people in recipient societies see of such programs comes in the form of relatively short-term, discreet efforts. It is at this level that most procedures are tied into the project cycle. Behind the reliance on projects is an assumption that, over time, if there are enough projects, they will add up to comprehensive and systemic change.

But as noted previously, many people in recipient societies observe that projects do not add up. In their experience, one project simply leads to other projects; they are often piecemeal interventions that are not strategic and cannot, with such limited time commitments, support systemic change. The point here is that many recipients identify the proceduralization of the processes of the project cycle (assessments, proposal writing, reporting) as contributing to and reinforcing the piecemeal nature of assistance. They call for more holistic approaches and long-term thinking that, they believe, would support sustainable impacts.

> 66 Many people criticized the "project mentality" among donors and aid agencies, saying that it lacked a long-term vision and impact and that more money was wasted with short-term thinking. Some noted that when projects are started by outsiders, the projects are often left to deteriorate and even called by the name of the "owners" (i.e., donors or NGO). People were critical of how most projects do not help communities identify their own resources and how to build on them. 99
>
> - Listening Project Report, Kenya

2. Principle of Equitableness

Aid providers set criteria by which to decide where and when to provide assistance. In doing so, many weigh two factors: they want to be strategic, and they want to be equitable. We saw above that people in recipient societies feel that aid is not sufficiently strategic but, too often, comes as piecemeal projects. Regarding equitableness, they note that aid as a delivery system largely focuses on overcoming perceived disadvantages (i.e., supporting equitableness) by addressing "needs." Recipients say that since aid is provided to address gaps in societies, providers often focus on those who have been marginalized economically, socially, and politically.

An Intrinsic Distortion?

Needs-based (gaps-based) programming, however, can distort the procedures used to do contextual analysis. The approach virtually obviates the potential for identifying and honoring existing capacities. When international assistance is meant to meet needs, aid agency procedures focus on identifying what is missing. They attempt to deliver material and nonmaterial aid to overcome the identified gaps.

As noted elsewhere, even though the language of "capacity building" is regularly used by donors and operational agencies, capacity building is often focused on meeting the "need" for "missing" capacities. Proposal frameworks and funding templates more often ask for evidence of "needs" that will be addressed by a proposed program rather than for evidence of capacities that the programs will support and reinforce.

The procedures aid providers most often use to determine who they should target with their assistance are essentially the same ones we discussed in relation to participation, ownership, and sustainability. The ways in which they affect distribution, however, deserve specific examination.

Preplanning for Proposals and Funding Purposes

The necessity of specifying (some would say "over-specifying") "targets" in order to get funding locks agencies into preset distribution criteria. Because this specification occurs before funded activities can begin, these may or may not turn out to be the right targets under local conditions. The proposal/funding nexus as it presets reporting criteria makes adjustments for local conditions difficult. To receive funding and be seen as "efficient and effective," agencies accept the limits of their preset plans, often to the detriment of more successful outcomes. Space for people in recipient communities to provide input on how to allocate resources in the early stages of planning is, in these procedures of proposing and funding, marginal or nonexistent.

Though donors and agencies affirm their commitment to meeting local needs or addressing missing capacities, many people on the recipient side of assistance say that aid is distributed according to the requirements of donors and agencies rather than according to local priorities and needs.

Assessment Procedures

Assessment procedures also lead to problematic distributional decisions. The standardized procedures most agencies use to determine who should receive their assistance assess whether or not people in any given community *need* what they, as an agency, have to offer. Agencies seldom are free to open their inquiry widely—looking for capacities (as noted above) or listening to options and ideas local people offer. Assessment tools are designed to document findings and structure local responses in templates, frameworks, models, and categories that are related to the mandates and specialties of the aid agency doing the assessment. (This in part, explains why each agency feels it must do its own needs assessment rather than relying on those done by others.)

> " Many people did not understand the criteria for assistance of different projects and did not get explanations as to why some people and communities were assisted while others were not. Many said that people were targeted differently under different projects of different agencies and that the criteria often were inconsistent and did not make sense. Many people noted that each organization did its own assessments, had its own information and did not seem to share this. "
>
> - Listening Project Report, Bosnia-Herzegovina

Assessment procedures designed to convince donors that what an aid agency is good at doing is exactly what people in a given region need are, by their very nature, too "closed" to capture the range of opinions and options offered by local people.

Fair or Unfair?

People in many locations say that they do not understand the procedures for setting distribution criteria. Procedures for "consultation" are, it seems, more extractive than informative. That is, they are designed (and followed) to gather information about what people need or want more than to communicate back to people about why the agency made specific decisions. In particular, people say they are not told how aid agencies use what they learn through surveys to determine where and to whom to provide aid. Because the terms on which some people receive aid and others do not are unclear, to many they seem unfair.

People say that because the categories and templates are not appropriate for their circumstances, the result is misallocation and waste of international donors' resources. For example, in some areas, people say that it is right for aid to be provided to widows and orphans, while in other areas, people say that larger families should be the focus. The issue is context. Standardized procedures for determining aid allocations seem to under-assess variations in circumstances and cultures.

Perverse Incentives

Some people raise another aspect of beneficiary selection procedures that they feel undermines effective assistance. This has to do with disincentives for people to move out of the recipient categories. In general, procedural categories do not include designations that leave room for people to transition from dependency to independency. One result is that people fight to retain benefits, even though they also wish to be independent. Some recipients suggest that processes be developed that help people move from an aid target category into increasing levels of self-reliance, rather than have clear lines of demarcation between eligibility and ineligibility for support from, or relationship with, assistance providers.

" No matter how much of a gang member a youth may be, he is a person who wants to move forward in his life. This is why I don't understand why the people that help continue to call us gang members. A gang member is helped in order that he stops being a gang member, but then he receives no help if he's not a gang member. "

- Young former male gang member, Ecuador

Consultation Processes

And people say, consultation processes, again, often fail to correct distributional misjudgments because there are limited opportunities for agency staff to listen to a wide range of inputs from people in recipient societies.

Western concepts of vulnerability and worthiness do not always match local concepts. For minority ethnic groups in Cambodia, who stated that they believe everyone is equal and deserves the same aid, foreign concepts of vulnerability clashed with local concepts of fairness. "They come and ask about our needs and then come with district officials to distribute.... We don't agree with the selection. Poverty assessment is based on whether or not the family owns a motorbike or a wooden house (richer) or no motorbike and bamboo house (poorer)." People were angered by the selection criteria and stormed out of the community meeting. (Listening Project Report, Cambodia)

"They decided to give bread to the displaced, but only to families with more than four members. This is not logical. The ones who really need it are the widows, the old couple who is living alone without relatives. The big families usually have members who can work."
(Refugee in a camp, Lebanon)

The lack of transparency regarding criteria for selecting beneficiaries was the cause of discontent in many areas in Zimbabwe. In only a minority of cases were community members aware of how beneficiary selections were decided. Often the outcomes made obvious the distortions that had occurred, including one example where bedridden people were given agricultural tools. (Listening Project Report, Zimbabwe)

"We know there should be priorities (often named by villagers as 'weak and widows' or 'poor and alone' or 'those who lost the most') but the tenth priority gets things while the first does not." (Villager, Indonesia)

Some people in Angola complained about the targeting of widows and elderly persons for assistance, saying that the neediest families were those with the most mouths to feed, which in many cases, did not meet any of the various official selection criteria for "vulnerability." There was general discomfort with the relatively low age of 50 used by some aid agencies as the threshold for assistance to the elderly. As one apparently healthy woman in Luanda observed, "I am 48; am I almost elderly?" (Listening Project Report, Angola)

Some NGOs said that they often have to design programs without specific communities in mind, then later are assigned communities by the government, making it difficult to meet the specific needs of selected communities. (Listening Project Report, Ethiopia)

"Here in San Lorenzo, I know of programs that call on people who know that help was being provided only for them to be in the picture for the final report." (Afro-Ecuadorian youth member of a CBO, Ecuador)

There were comments about NGOs promising or feigning a participatory approach but in fact acting in a fashion that was quite different. This includes NGOs relying too much on local leaders (sometimes a single leader) who themselves did not consult widely and openly and who dealt with others in an authoritarian manner. (Listening Project Report, Bolivia)

3. The Principle of Mutual Accountability

Finally, donors and recipients alike are committed to accountability. They agree on the importance of the principle, and they agree that procedures can be useful for promoting accountability.

Donors rely principally on narrative and financial reports to determine that their assistance has been delivered honestly and without mismanagement, that the original target population has been served, and that original goals have been achieved. Reports are written by consultants, international and national staff in charge of projects, local partner organizations and, occasionally, by someone in a recipient community. Reporting procedures have been tightened according to each donor's needs (which do not always correspond!) throughout the international assistance system.

Procedures have also been developed to ensure that donors and aid agencies are accountable to people in recipient societies. Some agencies welcome "audits" in which external agencies assess their professionalism and reliability according to international standards of delivery through field visits. Some agencies use suggestions or complaints boxes, inviting people in recipient communities to provide anonymous feedback—positive and negative—about their efforts. Some try to elicit honest recipient judgments through community meetings and monitoring and evaluation tools.[9]

But there is widely shared agreement among many people in recipient communities that these procedures for mutual accountability (to both donors and recipients) are largely failing.

Narrative and Financial Reporting

Aid providers and receivers both say that current report-writing procedures, completely counter to their intent, introduce inefficiencies into international assistance work. Report preparation to meet donor requirements to ensure continued funding for a series of projects becomes an end in itself. Aid agencies say that more and more of their time is spent complying with reporting requirements in each successive year. The costs of reporting have, many feel, overtaken the value of reporting—particularly as the procedures of reporting limit the scope of what is covered to "results" that were specified in proposals rather than encouraging engagement with people on accountability around actual impacts and learning that can improve future performance.

Four problems with the proceduralization of reports are identified and discussed at length by people (aid recipients and aid workers) who live and work in recipient countries.

Reports focus on what was proposed, not on what actually happened.

To track that funds have been spent to achieve what was proposed, donors ask aid agencies (and recipients) to prove that they engage in "results-based management." Donors require reports that are tied directly to the proposals they funded to justify and account for their provision of funds. This limits flexibility and responsiveness to contextual changes. It may mean that actual results (not proposed) are not included in reports.

---

[9] See the Listening Project report on "Feedback Mechanisms in International Assistance Organizations" on the CDA website (2011).

> " For international donors, a project is only useful if it has immediate results that they can show and measure. How can you heal a trauma in six months? And tell me how can you take a picture of a healed trauma? "
>
> - Coordinator of a Lebanese NGO, Lebanon

Reports are overly complicated.

In an effort to streamline reporting, many donors and aid agencies have developed standardized formats. Perversely, most users of these formats (from large international NGOs to small, local community-based organizations) say that such standardized formats have made reporting more complicated rather than simpler. Many also note that standardized formats limit honesty and accountability by predetermining reporting categories rather than inviting genuine reflection on what has occurred. This relates also to the "faking" of reports; people say that as much is left out of such set formats as is included in them. The complications also make it more difficult for local people to be involved in reporting.

Reports often are untrue; they do not in fact promote accountability.

People comment on three aspects of the dishonesty of reports. First, because reports focus only on what was proposed, so much may be left out that they represent very little of the reality. Second, many note it is easy to provide pictures (sometimes faked) and receipts (also sometimes faked) to meet reporting requirements since it is widely known that donors will not often go to the field to see what has or has not occurred. Third, many people note with frustration that a true report would include the ideas and analyses of people in recipient communities about the larger impacts of any activity. Most people were quite clear that they are not consulted or listened to about lasting impacts. Most feel that they have no way to hold international assistance providers accountable for impacts in their locations. Not all want to complain, but they do want to have an opportunity to provide feedback that is heeded. This is not accomplished by current reporting procedures.

The message is that donor agencies do not really care about real impacts or lasting results, but only about reports.

Perhaps the most pernicious effect of the proceduralization of reporting is the message it sends to people in recipient societies. Many say they doubt the sincerity of the international assistance community's claims to want to be helpful. Instead, they say, the system is self-serving: it is interlinked through proposals that get funding that lead to top-down and prepackaged programming, which is then reported on as successful when it delivers the things that outsiders decided it should deliver. It is, people feel, more concerned with its self-perpetuation than with actual outcomes and impacts. Their cynicism about the purposes of aid is reinforced by standardized reporting procedures that do not capture their voices, reflect real events, or provide a basis for increased understanding and development of alternatives. In short, current reporting procedures have become so proceduralized that they undermine, rather than support, the principle of mutual accountability. This is, most feel, not only a travesty, but also a missed opportunity.

There was a general sense, especially among people who worked for Cambodian NGOs, that donors required too much in writing, both for reporting and for requesting funds. There was also frustration that reporting timelines and formats were not synchronized between donors so that some NGOs had to spend more time and effort writing progress reports rather than focusing on the projects. Paying only for project costs and not administration costs, and making project payments late, were also concerns to local NGOs. (Listening Project Report, Cambodia)

"There is no interest to develop people; it is all reduced to practicality. Just know how to write a report. The focus is on skills put into the framework of outputs with no reflection included."
(Director of a Local NGO, Lebanon)

The issue has to do with useful follow-up, such as participatory evaluation at the end of a project and occasional monitoring or just checking in during the years after the active presence of the NGO has ended. One person added that it must be taken into account that donors rarely authorize an additional budget for monitoring or evaluation once the project ends, nor do executing institutions invest in carrying out such follow-up, which always has a cost. (Listening Project Report, Bolivia)

One person pointed out that NGO projects are often timeframe-oriented, rather than human-oriented; that projects occur only during the defined timeframe, whether or not the project objectives were achieved and were sustainable. (Listening Project Report, Myanmar/Burma)

Conclusion

Standard Procedures and Contextual Appropriateness: Compatible or Contradictory?

The international aid community is committed at both the policy and practice levels to the principles of good donorship. The principles discussed above emerged in response to what aid providers observed of the policy/program gap. Procedures were developed, standardized, and systematized first to make it impossible to ignore these principles and then to regularize their translation into field practice.

It is therefore challenging to hear people in aid-recipient societies analyze the missteps between aid providers' commitments and field-based outcomes. Does their commentary suggest that procedures should be abandoned?

Their answer—and ours—is a clear "No."

As noted, people in recipient societies also want the predictability and consistency that procedures can provide. What they want does not differ from what most donors and operational agencies also want—namely, standardized processes for ensuring that outsiders and insiders, in each context, can effectively engage together to promote peace and development.

If we listen to the analyses of people in recipient communities about their experiences with procedures, three notable factors emerge that point to solutions to the problems the current proceduralization generates.

First, the location and timing of many decisions about international assistance are undermining the very principles aid providers seek to pursue.

Second, the approach to assistance through projects with relatively limited funding cycles limits attainment of the principles.

Third, the focus of decisions and funding on the delivery of goods and services, with less attention to process—that is, the focus on what is done more than on how it is done—gets in the way of achieving the principles of good donorship.

When principles and procedures are over-elaborated as they have been, they undermine genuine relationship-building, which—most people in aid-recipient societies suggest—should be at the heart of effective international aid efforts. Procedures adopted to facilitate more effective and efficient international assistance have turned in on themselves and now, more often than not, undermine the purposes for which they were created. The international assistance enterprise needs processes that work. The challenge now is to dismantle those that are counterproductive and to find ways to develop new processes that accomplish their intent.

• • • • • • • • •

CHAPTER SEVEN

INTERNATIONAL ASSISTANCE IN PARTNERSHIP WITH GOVERNMENTS AND CIVIL SOCIETY

... in which we hear people insist that aid providers partner with existing institutions and, at the same time, raise serious concerns about what happens when they do so.

Existing Institutions: A Capacity

Every society, no matter how poor, has formal and informal arrangements through which people together make decisions and take action. These may be inclusive, representing broad interests, or hierarchical, favoring the elite. They may be national, operating at the state level, or they may be quite local, including people from one village or clan. Their structures vary widely, as do their strengths and weaknesses. Still, such structures provide the potential for an organizational mechanism for collective action. They are an existing capacity to be recognized by providers of international assistance.

The idea of partnering with local and national organizations is important in international aid efforts. There is wide agreement that outside aid providers should work through existing institutions where they are strong and support them, if weak, to help them gain experience and resources for bettering their societies. Receivers and providers of aid together recognize that international donors are only temporary actors in recipient societies and that governments and local organizations know their contexts better than outsiders do.

Partnerships have become the mechanism through which international assistance agencies work with and through formal and informal local structures to "build" or support capacities to ensure that recipient countries can sustain progress after the assistance ends. As noted, the apparatus of the international assistance system is multilayered. In this chapter, we look at the ways that international assistance providers pursue partnerships with two of these "layers" on the recipient side— governments and civil society organizations.

What People Say

People in recipient communities feel strongly that international assistance should connect to and strengthen their governments and civil society. They urge outsiders to partner with local structures, and they are highly critical of aid that bypasses their institutions.

At the same time, people in recipient societies express concerns that the partnerships of donors and aid agencies with their governments and civil society have severe limitations and, sometimes, negative effects.

Two factors are key to understanding their concerns. First, context matters. The histories and experiences of people's interactions with their governments and civil society organizations shape their judgments about how international assistance should, or should not, engage with these entities. Second, a generally perceived asymmetry of power between givers and receivers affects peoples' judgments about partnering. Many feel that the relationship between external aid providers and internal aid receivers involves a dynamic of innate or expected inequality. When most policies, procedures, and decisions originate from outside and assistance arrives in the form of pre-packaged programs, as occurs in the externally driven delivery system approach, people feel that outside priorities and agendas overpower local priorities and realities. The evidence they offer shows that partnerships are not easy—for either aid provider or aid recipient.

Partnerships with Governments: How Context Matters
History of Distrust

In societies where poverty and/or conflict are widespread—that is, in the very societies where international aid frequently focuses—it is often the case that people do not have high confidence in their governments. In their daily struggles, they see little evidence that their government is sincere in promoting their welfare. They don't feel they have access to existing structures or that politicians hear their concerns. Many speak of their distrust of government from local to national level.

> 66 Aid very often does not reach the targeted population. And when it does arrive, it's just crumbs. Most of the assistance is blocked in the offices of the central administration and evaporates into nature. The question I ask is: why do the donors continue to pour money [into the government] in this context? Do they really want to contribute to the improvement in the standard of living of vulnerable populations in Mali? If so, they need to change their strategy and listen attentively to the targeted population. 99
> - Manager of a state-owned enterprise in Mali

International donors are increasingly providing aid to and through governmental channels as a way of strengthening good governance. When citizens distrust their governments and perceive them with cynicism, this strategy evokes concern. Their deep-seated concerns based on past experience influence local people's assessments of the benefits and negative consequences of international assistance.

> **"Government departments promise but do not deliver. The government sector is far behind the NGOs in regard to assistance. They are good at lip service but not with delivery."** (A rural group, Thailand)

> **Afghan people often commented on the way power structures at the national and at the community levels influenced the process of aid distribution, beneficiary selection, project implementation, and the long-term results. In Kabul, most people referred to the national government structures, while in the provinces, people talked about local power structures. People spoke about favoritism in the decision-making process and their distrust for authorities—both traditional and the new government structures. Recipients of assistance and non-recipients both questioned whether external assistance is promoting transparent forms of governance or reinforcing the existing opaque structures.**
> (Listening Project Report, Afghanistan)

> **The main reason why middle persons are seen as problematic is the issue of corruption. There is a perception that somewhere along the way, money gets diverted by people for their own purposes, or for the benefit of a specific group of people. Many people point to the political party in particular, saying that Members of Parliament distribute these funds only to the people who are supporting them, or that many of these funds do not reach the people at all.** (Listening Project Report, Solomon Islands)

> **Many people said that local governments were not transparent and did not communicate well with local communities. They complained that elected officials are focused on serving their political party interests more than serving the citizens' interests. Some said that the government structure set up by the international community just creates more government jobs, higher taxes, more bureaucracy, and makes it more difficult to coordinate, collaborate and get things done.**
> (Listening Project Report, Bosnia-Herzegovina)

Corruption and Favoritism

People's distrust of government sometimes entails specific allegations of corruption and favoritism. A number of people note that the resources provided by the international assistance community can be, and often are, "siphoned off" by government officials for their own purposes. (See Chapter 8 on corruption for a fuller discussion of this issue.)

> " People don't receive assistance. When it's given through government ministries, all the ministries take that money and people are being neglected. Just to send details to donors, [government officials] come and take some photos, and say that they have provided all the money to the community and the donors believe that. "
>
> - Bus driver, Sri Lanka

Politicization

People in multiple locations describe how government officials use international assistance to achieve or maintain political power. In some places, this kind of politicization of assistance is simply accepted as inevitable; in others, it generates real anger toward national and local politicians. (This issue is also further discussed in Chapter 8 on corruption.) Where agencies provide aid to an un-trusted or oppressive government, people conclude that international aid providers are complicit in the politicization of aid.

> " If you are from the opposite party, you will get no aid to develop your area. And the ruling party will accuse the other parties of not helping people. Aid is manipulated for political favor and to disfavor other political parties. Foreign assistance is used to show that the ruling party is generous. "
>
> - Local NGO staff, Cambodia

In many places, a historical distrust of government couples with experiences of diversion, corruption, and politicization of aid to define the government-citizenry nexus that is the context for international assistance partnerships. When outsiders engage with governmental bodies and channel funds through them, they can be seen to support poor governance. When external aid providers fail to acknowledge this context or assume that their aid can in some automatic or deliberate way help it change, they miss the contextual challenge. From the judgments of many in recipient societies, aid providers' partnerships with governments require something more than recipients now observe. One influencing factor that they name is the intrinsic inequality between donor and recipient.

"We will never complain to the government again. I think the government makes corruption and takes the support away from us. We feel a loss of confidence with these people; we will make no more contact with them." (An old woman who is an IDP, Timor-Leste)

"There is a lot of politics at play when governments get involved. Projects are given to friends." (The director of an agency within a national ministry, Ecuador)

In Bolivia, people commented on the role of local leaders in the allocation process. Several people said aid was not getting to the people because NGOs depend too much on one or a few leaders who are not always trusted by the people. (Listening Project Report, Bolivia)

"Most resettled people were Sinhala. The government used international assistance to change demographics." (Community leader, Sri Lanka)

"The same 'war politics' is driving who gets aid today, with politicians only helping their own people." (Community members, Bosnia-Herzegovina)

"Government and NGOs are brothers in corruption. Look at the highway—it cost more than $1 million and it is falling apart. Money has been spent but it has been wasted. The origin of the problem is lack of honesty of agencies.... NGOs bypass the government. NGOs do not understand our needs. The government knows but is not honest."
(University faculty member, Afghanistan)

In Ethiopia, a few people intimated that NGOs that closely cooperate with the government are not seen as impartial, especially by those who do not support the current government or who are unhappy with the targeting of assistance. An urban resident said that "NGOs follow the interest of the national government and focus on rural areas" (as opposed to the urban areas, which are not the base for the ruling party). (Listening Project Report, Ethiopia)

"If you leave resource allocation up to the Lebanese government, everything is politicized, everything is politically driven, and everything is communal." (Member of Parliament, Lebanon)

> "The UN and donors work through the government, even though the government does not reflect the needs of the people. Water, for example, is a basic necessity but not a national priority. Whether it's true or not, we have to follow the project goals of the government. That is the UN mandate. How much the government reflects the interest of the people is a different issue." (UN staff member, Timor-Leste)

> "Not all 100% of aid reaches to the ground level. Only 25% reaches the community because of government restrictions."
> (Businessman in a remote state, Myanmar/Burma)

Partnerships with Governments: How Inequality Matters

Government officials in recipient societies comment both on the intrusive and overpowering donor approaches that impose external priorities and on international donors' failure to be sufficiently present and involved in the delivery of assistance. These seem to be contradictory complaints—one seeking less interventionism and the other seeking more. However, both reflect the fact that recipient governments often feel unable to affect the contours and quality of their relationships with aid providers. Many say they either "take what is offered" or refuse it, but that they do not have the kind of relationship they would value in partnership.[10]

Not surprisingly, international aid providers look for reliable governments to partner with because they do not want to make the mistakes outlined above—namely, feed into corruption, be complicit with oppression, or condone politicization of aid. However, donor choices about which governments to partner with are seen in some places as misguided. This occurs, they say, when providers bypass and fail to support incompetent agencies of otherwise effective governments and when national governments that are widely seen as pariahs are internationally shunned. For example, in the Philippines, people say that an international donor bias for working with effective local government units is ill-conceived because it is precisely weak governments that most need external help. In Zimbabwe, villagers say that donor decisions to avoid their government consign them to exclusion from the world's assistance and that it is precisely because their government fails them that they so need international assistance and the presence of outsiders.

---

[10] The Paris Declaration on Aid Effectiveness, the Accra Agenda for Action, and the Busan Partnership for Effective Development Cooperation acknowledge the need for better relationships between donors and recipients of aid to make aid more effective. However, many of the principles that have been agreed on have not been implemented in practice, as noted in the Paris Declaration Monitoring Surveys and the Fragile States Principles Surveys in 2011.

"Those areas of Mindanao that have capable government units receive outside funding while others where local government is perceived as weak do not, even though the areas that have weak governance need more support and capacity building. This preference to work with strong government units stems in part from donors' need to meet reporting requirements and those local government units with the capacity to articulate their needs are often the same ones that can provide the reports required by donors. Similarly the local NGOs and CBOs with large enough capacity to implement projects are often the only ones able to meet stringent donor reporting requirements."
(Members of Listening Team, Philippines)

"Often, an offer of donor funds arrives suddenly without prior notice and at any time of the year. It usually comes with requirements for the contribution of an economic counterpart and the only source is the municipality. This situation causes conflicts when resources have to be taken from one community in order to make them available for another one. This is due to the fact that the Annual Operative Plan with its respective assigning of funds for communities and for specific activities is decided upon at the end of the year, for the following year."
(Mayor's chief assistant, Bolivia)

"The donors have different agendas and these are directed from their own headquarters. They are listening less to the Afghan government. The case with the Provincial Reconstruction Teams (PRTs) is worse, where each PRT is different and is guided by military objectives without following the Provincial Development Strategies." (Government representative, Afghanistan)

"Our superiors tell us to support projects that are implemented in our districts or villages because the plans have been determined at the national level. But this means we have little local input. We want to be more involved in project design. We remain dependent on NGOs due to lack of capacity and resources to sustain projects after they are handed over to the government or communities. (Government official, Ethiopia)

Partnerships with Civil Society: How Context Matters

Effective partnerships with civil society organizations are also difficult for some of the same, and some different, reasons. Again, context matters. People in aid-recipient societies report that civil society groups, like governments, sometimes misuse resources and engage in corruption and favoritism. They describe mismanagement, ineptitude, and self-enrichment by staff of some civil society organizations.

For their part, civil society leaders struggle with competing demands and expectations. In societies where traditions dictate strong familial and clan allegiances, these leaders are caught in the middle. Leaders of local organizations who receive donor support are locally expected to follow the norms of clan loyalty. And, they are expected by donor partners to act without bias or favoritism.

> 66 Villagers in Aceh often referred to diversion of goods by chiefs of villages and other governmental authorities. They noted that local staff of international NGOs tend to favor friends or relatives but acknowledged that even if they want to follow international rules and treat everyone the same, their families expect them to help them first. Some emphasized the responsibility of international NGOs by noting that local staff were "not to blame because they are not professional, they have not been trained" by their employers. 99
>
> - Listening Project Report, Indonesia

In societies where authorities have always undervalued or restricted civil society, local organizations—often formed by international aid providers—lack experience and are not fully aware of the roles of civil society. In countries where local NGOs have provided the only non-biased humanitarian aid to people during civil war and have consistently maintained distance from governmental authorities, these NGOs find themselves in uncharted territory when their post-conflict government resumes provision of services. When indigenous NGOs have been the watchdogs and critics of oppressive governance, they do not find it easy to engage with a reforming government. Partnerships of outside donors with local groups are colored by such contextual differences.

Partnerships with Civil Society: How Inequality Matters

When international aid providers are concerned with delivery of assistance, their partnerships with civil society organizations mirror that of a company and its middlemen. Relations of aid providers with local organizations often are focused on distributing goods and services provided through outside assistance more than on engaging colleagues in problem solving. People in recipient societies—including those in the local organizations that are the "partners" of external donors—report two problems.

"Middlemen" Use Up Resources

First, some people want all aid to come directly to communities rather than through intermediaries such as CBOs and NGOs because they see how intermediaries use ("siphon off") the resources that local communities feel they need. "Middlemen" are consumers of aid as well as conduits for it. They hire staff and have administrative costs that people do not think adds value to the aid process.

At the same time, local organizations often feel that they are "used" by international donors to deliver goods but that they have little influence on how to allocate resources or decide what is actually done. Even when local NGOs are seen to function effectively, some people feel that they are just one more layer in the delivery system that requires funding to operate—meaning that fewer resources actually reach intended beneficiaries. When civil society partners are seen only as middlemen for assistance, many communities simply want to do without them.

> 66 Can aid come to the beneficiaries without going through the many middlemen and reach the people whole—the way it was given by the donor? For example, a new bottle of water is full, how best can it come down to the people without being opened on the way? Let aid come to the grassroots! 99
>
> - Leader of a women's group, Kenya

Local NGOs and CBOs Become Defined Only as Agents of Aid

Second, civil society organizations in recipient societies say that their partnerships with external donors turn them into agents of assistance rather than independent civil society actors. They become dependent on external funding (not local contributions), and they mirror the system that developed them—that is, the international aid agencies. Much of the "capacity-building" provided to recipient society organizations teaches them to write proposals (for external funds) and to report according to donor demands. That is, rather than becoming independent civic entities addressing local problems with local people, they are appealing to external donors (and responding to external donor agendas) for their continued existence.

> 66 A project society has been developed, not a civil society. 99
>
> - Researcher and policy advisor, Kosovo

International aid agencies develop partnerships with local groups with the intent of helping to strengthen civil society. Some operate from a notion of how societies "should" function with power shared between a democratic government and independent non-governmental organizations. In approaching support to civil society this way, some aid agencies are in essence "delivering" a societal model based on their own national experience. Even though many elements of such a model may apply in other locations, the importation of a model from one context to another, especially when it is backed by funding from giver to receiver, can represent an inequality between the societal model's originator and its recipient. Again, context and inequality shape how aid provider–civil society partnerships do or do not work.

"We feel like INGOs come and order us to do things this way or that because they have a lot of power ... we don't see a lot of working together in a meaningful way.... We want real partnership. For this we must always have open dialogue and mutual respect. The CBOs should not look like service providers or staff for NGOs. CBOs should have more role and voice for social change."
(Leader of a CBO in a refugee camp, Thai–Burma border)

"We are not happy with local NGOs because people in international NGOs give money to local NGOs to implement programs but they don't do their work well. They use up the money too quickly or just throw it away." (Villagers in a remote area, Timor-Leste)

"Local NGOs need to be more accountable as well. They always try and hide costs and to justify conferences and nights over in five-star hotels."
(Rural community member, Sri Lanka)

"Some NGOs are doing humanitarian work as a business, like a super-profit-one-man-show. There is one local person who knows how to deal with donors, and he or she fixes the projects for the international community according to the donor priorities. These NGOs work on demand, depending on what the current donor agenda is. NGOs are like mushrooms, when the climate changes, they shoot out of the ground."
(Local researcher, Lebanon)

Out in several provinces of Afghanistan, people pointed to a number of ways that valuable aid resources are siphoned off, mismanaged, stolen, etc. One example was about a literacy course funded and implemented by one of the international organizations, which failed to deliver the stationery required for the students taking the classes. The course did not commence until the Education Department provided the stationery out of their funds. The shura member said, "I am sure that the staff use the stationery for themselves. Notebooks with the agency logo on them are sold in the markets. They are gifts from the agency and intended for communities, but the staff sell them." (Listening Project Report, Afghanistan)

> Competition among NGO staff to be hired and then to have power, influence, and control over institutional resources can create scenarios of corruption and unethical values. High NGO salaries and lack of information generate mistrust among the beneficiaries and are perceived by them as unethical to the point where there are cases of communities rejecting NGO staff, sometimes violently. (Listening Project Report, Ecuador)

> Some people said that a lot of money was lost or wasted through the typical funding mechanism—flowing from the donors to international NGOs to local NGOs—which resulted in higher overhead and operational costs. Some people were concerned about the sustainability of local NGOs since so many are still project-driven and dependent on donor funding. (Listening Project Report, Bosnia-Herzegovina)

In Spite of All This, International Aid Providers Should Partner with Local Institutions Anyway!

In spite of the difficulties with donor/government partnerships, people both within and outside of government feel that aid providers have a responsibility to connect with existing governance structures. And, even though people name a number of problems they see when donor funds come through local NGOs and CBOs, they nonetheless urge donors to continue partnering with civil society groups. People in aid-receiving societies clearly want international assistance efforts to connect to, and reinforce, strengthen, or improve, their existing collective institutional capacities.

People note that when international assistance bypasses government and goes directly to communities, government bodies are unprepared to continue with and support the activities begun by international agencies when these agencies leave. Sometimes, they are simply unwilling to do so because these activities were not in line with their priorities and because they resent the fact that they were bypassed. They identify such projects as belonging to the NGOs, and many government officials do not feel ownership or responsibility over the future of these initiatives.

In some areas, there is special criticism for aid providers who focus only on building civil society and, therefore, deprive governmental entities of needed support. Especially in post-conflict areas, people say that their governments are overwhelmed and that short-term international support that does not connect to government structures can undermine both the authority and the competence-building of such governments. This can endanger state-building efforts and fragile post-conflict peace.

> 66 If you work with the local government you build more capacity and ensure sustainability. We've learned our lessons from mistakes we made. In the past, we focused almost entirely on village-based or community-based organizations, trained local village committees to write proposals and apply for funding. After we phased out, these committees fell apart because they didn't have a proper network with the local government. 99
>
> - Local staff of an INGO, Sri Lanka

People in recipient societies also want international assistance to help them develop civil, non-formal mechanisms for meeting community priorities. Some urge this help for civil society organizations rather than partnering with governments; others urge it on its own merits. Many cite examples of positive impacts of donor-civil society partnerships that they hope will be enlarged.

> 66 There is a tendency of donors to seek local offices to avoid intermediation, but sometimes they become competitors of the NGOs. External aid should promote the local capacities of NGOs, not compete with them. We believe that the donor organizations have made a mistake in avoiding the NGOs in order to go directly to the beneficiaries. 99
>
> - Staff member of an NGO, Ecuador

While people in all places agreed that international aid should support civil society and strengthen good governance, important variations occurred in how people thought about the role of assistance in relation to their governments. These variations reflect the vastly different experiences people have with their governments, shaped by their histories of conflict, despotism, instability, or marginalization. It becomes obvious that neither people in countries in transition *nor* international actors really know how to move from inadequate, weak, and self-serving governments toward improving, competent, and responsive governance.

International policy documents call for support of "good governance" but do not specify the steps between "here" and "there." In spite of many efforts, international aid providers do not have a clear understanding of how best to engage with bad governments *so that progress toward good governance is supported*. This is an area where experience (good and bad) could be gathered and compared to see what lessons can be learned. It also helps explain why aid provider-government partnerships are so difficult.

"Having coordination meetings is important. Some NGOs implement programs and don't let the ministry know. This is a problem because the projects become the government's responsibility when they are over." (Ministry official, Timor-Leste)

"You could even say that the big international institutes are 'crowding out' the government. The government is weak in Lebanon, they are taking over some of its functions and thereby they weaken it instead of strengthening it" (Government representative, Lebanon)

"A problem occurs when projects are handed over to the government, as in the case of a water supply system, and the government has no idea what to do with them because the implementing agency did not seek permission or include the government in planning." (Provincial government official, Sri Lanka)

"Foreign aid organizations don't trust the government to manage the funds transparently, but they don't train us how to do it right. Providing the training is more important so that the work can be sustained once the outside organization leaves." (Government official, Cambodia)

"Afghan NGOs are better than foreigners because they understand our problems."(Head of a Community Development Committee, Afghanistan)

"NGO intervention is more important because they are more efficient and they are 'seen' in the community, unlike the government. NGOs have good outputs, auditing, and accountability." (Vice Principal of a school, Sri Lanka)

An alternative model is used by some financial agencies, which changes the entire dynamic between the beneficiaries and the NGOs. In this model, the grassroots organizations hire technical assistance when needed and for the time needed. It is not only cheaper, but it totally transforms the relationship between technicians and beneficiaries— from donors and supplicants to persons who contract and those that are contracted. (Listening Project Report, Bolivia)

A number of people in Bosnia said that the development of local NGOs has had a positive impact in Bosnia, especially by increasing women's participation in the sphere of politics. Many beneficiaries said they were more satisfied with the assistance they received from local NGOs than the assistance they got from international NGOs because the former are enmeshed in the problems of the country and can thus better understand and serve people's needs. Some said that when local NGOs have the same capacity, they should be preferred by donors over international NGOs because they cost less and understand the needs of the community better.

(Listening Project Report, Bosnia-Herzegovina)

"The relational aspects of follow-up and accompaniment are important. Donor visits to the field reinforce relations with partners and communities since they provide a valuable opportunity to get to know one another, to listen, to discuss problems together and to find joint solutions."

(Local people, Mali)

Many people noted the history of distrust of outsiders and the need for outsiders to build relationships first in order to be effective.

(Listening Project Report, New Orleans, USA)

Follow-up to Improve Partnerships with Both Government and Civil Society

As they urge that international aid providers continue to pursue partnerships with both government and civil society in spite of the problems encountered, many people also call for more oversight and follow-up by donors and aid agencies. This would, they say, prevent misuse of funds and provide more opportunities for building relationships. They strongly emphasize collegiality, mutual respect, and joint problem solving—as opposed to outward dependency on external funding, agendas, and ideas.

> " International aid had come in three phases: 1) gifts ... but not in bad faith; 2) how to improve life-styles, which is not sustainable in either time or place; and 3) [as happens now] joint planning, joint diagnosis, capacity to give opinions and propose things, the training of local people. "
>
> - Provincial Council leader, Ecuador

Aid recipients expect aid providers to know who they are partnering with and to trust (and verify) that they are providing assistance effectively. Recipients acknowledge that the balance between trust and control is important in effective partnership. When international partners arrive for unannounced visits, their local partners may think that they do not trust them. However, local people point out that things can easily be "arranged" when an international agency notifies a partner or community of its visit beforehand. Several people suggested that, "trust does not exclude control," and that monitoring one's partners need not reflect a lack of confidence or diminish the spirit of partnership. Instead, they believe that if aid providers evaluate their partners and their partnerships regularly, this should truly improve accountability and build trust between aid providers and recipients.

Some people cite positive examples of how effective partnerships have strengthened government and civil society entities. They point to the importance of being familiar with the context, and how this matters to mutual understanding between aid providers and recipients. Others speak of the duration and consistency of contact that, over time, creates trusting relationships. Many talk about the amount of responsibility placed on local entities (representing respect and trust) as a factor that enables them to grow stronger, using partnership skills to accomplish broader goals within their societies.

> **Some donors in Mali who provide direct budgetary support acknowledged that there is pressure from their head offices to disburse funds quickly and that they have little time for visits to the field because of meetings in the capital and administrative obligations to their headquarters. Many people wondered whether donors were complicit in fostering corruption since they know very well what is going on with budgetary support and have not established proper monitoring mechanisms.**
> (Listening Project Report, Mali)

> **Some local government officials in Bosnia acknowledged that there had been problems and that they needed to do a better job in monitoring returns themselves, but noted that often donors and NGOs did not coordinate or involve them in the planning process, but then relied on them to provide the services and mediate the disputes which arose.**
> (Listening Project Report, Bosnia-Herzegovina)

> **Some communities perceived it as potentially dangerous to approach major international organizations because they are closely monitored by the government and this could attract attention to the community.**
> (Listening Project Report, Myanmar/Burma)

Conclusion

A delivery system approach to international assistance does not lend itself to healthy partnerships. Top-down decision-making, constraints on time and pre-specified funding commitments, pre-planning of projects, pre-identification of beneficiaries, and the proceduralization of approaches all concentrate power in the giver and limit adaptation to context. One-size-fits-all approaches undermine healthy relationships and, therefore, effective partnerships.

No generalizable formula exists for good donor-government or donor-civil society partnerships. In the aid system, these partnerships are complex and layered. Context matters and equality matters. Of necessity, a healthy partnership must be developed by all parties, over time and with focused effort. Partnerships in international assistance are too often seen as a means to an end (how to get the resources delivered). The commentary of people on the receiving end makes clear that partnerships are not just mechanisms for accomplishing donor purposes; developing healthy partnerships could be and should be a direct objective of effective aid. More meaningful and effective interaction between and among partners can, itself, produce progress toward the other goals of aid.

• • • • • • • • • •

CHAPTER EIGHT

CORRUPTION:
A SURPRISINGLY BROAD DEFINITION

... in which we hear different descriptions of corruption, learn that many procedures to end corruption do not work, and are told by aid recipients that aid providers should do more and be better at curbing it.

> “There was widespread agreement that international assistance would be more effective if corruption were reduced. Project designs, budgets and strategies should be openly shared and more transparent so that communities themselves can play a role in monitoring implementation.”
>
> - Listening Project Report, Mali

Introduction

Corruption is a troubling issue for people in all the countries the Listening Project visited. Across cultures and locations, differences of definition and manifestation exist, but everywhere, people describe legally corrupt practices and others they see as morally and ethically corrupt. One of the standard definitions of corruption—abuse of entrusted power for personal gain—makes it clear why these practices are antithetical to the purposes of international assistance.

From personal experience, people in recipient countries tell many stories of theft and diversion of aid's resources. They talk about unfair distribution systems that benefit people who are well-connected through favoritism, nepotism, and patronage. Some people say that these systems are endemic to their traditions and societies, and, therefore, they accept them as inevitable and unchangeable. Some explain why it occurs and express a degree of sympathy and understanding for the people who gain through it.

Beyond the unambiguous manifestations of corruption through theft, diversion, and unfair distribution, people often raise three other issues. These are aspects of international assistance that they see as "corrupting influences" that appear to condone endemic local corruption or, in some cases, even feed it and worsen it. These include what people see as extravagant spending or needless waste by international aid agencies and their staff, the delivery of too much aid (too quickly), and the absence of serious or effective accountability in aid efforts.

Theft and Diversion

> 66 Corruption is a standard operating procedure. A percentage is skimmed off the top of any project by everyone involved. Contractors get richer because of international aid. 99
>
> - Civic leader, Philippines

People in recipient countries tell many stories of theft and diversion of international aid. These stories often involve direct experience of a person skimming off a portion (sometimes quite large) of aid's resources for personal or family use. In some cases, people report on their "suspicions" of such actions based not on direct knowledge, but on their perceptions that the aid has helped too few people or accomplished too little given the quantity of resources they know has been provided. Even if they cannot substantiate their suspicions, people are left with a pervasive sense of grievance that aid is being misused or misappropriated.

Bribery, Favoritism, Nepotism, and Patronage

Akin to direct theft and diversion, but often differentiated by people in their own communities, is the misuse of aid goods and funds by those who can control their distribution. Whereas people who have direct access to aid can steal or divert it for their own use, those who control its distribution not only are able to siphon some off for themselves; they also can (and often do) use this control to exert, maintain, or gain political or social power over others.

There are three issues here. First is the very direct opportunity for additional diversion offered to those who directly control the distribution of aid. They may, of course, steal the goods themselves; but instead, they often offer them to the "highest bidder," exacting bribes and/or other favors in return for preferential treatment.

> 66 Every organization is under the influence of local community elders and tribal leaders. Aid often ends up in their hands and is not distributed based on need. 99
>
> - Villager, Afghanistan

Second, family or clan group favoritism is common and entrenched in many places around the world. The avenues by which providers deliver aid to communities can, because of favoritism, mean that some who are needy are completely left out, some who have no need receive goods, and tensions or conflicts between groups can be exacerbated.

Third, and of concern to many, is the regular use of aid resources in politicized ways. The power of authorities to reward or punish those who agree or disagree respectively is troubling. When international agencies provide significant resources that government or other political leaders may use for their personal political or economic gain, these agencies are seen to be reinforcing political systems that their own citizenry mistrust.

> "If you are not a member of a political party or you do not have any friends or family in the municipal administration, then you struggle to get any assistance. You have to be a political party member to get any assistance."
>
> — Local man, Kosovo

"In this region, one NGO manager says he has 36 employees but he really just has 6 and he keeps the rest of the money for the 30 other people for himself." (Villager, Myanmar/Burma)

"There are many sacks of wheat coming to the community, and each should be 50 kg. In the end, they only weighed 40 kg, and 150 sacks were lost." (Villager, Afghanistan)

"This one international NGO is like the mafia. It invited proposals from one local community, and allegedly obtained some 2 million Euros from donors. But that local community was later told that this organization does not work in this region." (Community member, Kosovo)

"In small villages like mine, when an aid agency asks me to provide a list of 15 households with beneficiaries, I give them a list of 15. But we only have 13 families, so I add myself and my family members to the list as #14 and #15." (Village chief, Zimbabwe)

"You want to know about aid? I will just say one word to you: wasta, wasta, wasta." (Wasta is the colloquial Arabic term frequently used when speaking about the practice of using one's personal contacts to influence outcomes in one's favor.) (Shop-owner in a refugee camp, Lebanon)

"I applied three times for a cow, but I did not get it because I belong to a different religious community than the minister. If you have a leader from your religious sect in the government, he will bring you aid. If not, nobody will take care for you." (Villager, Lebanon)

"You have to know the right person for aid to get from point A to point B. Family and relatives are point B." (Local government official, Timor-Leste)

"Politicians use aid for their preferences because they get to decide who the beneficiaries are and they get to include their friends or family members, even if they aren't qualified for the aid. They accommodate people they know rather than the IDPs. The politicians are using it for their political ends; they are owning it as if the project is coming from them." (Teacher, Philippines)

"The political leadership directs outside funding to their home provinces. When donors come to the national government, they are also directed to particular provinces. Most INGOs are concentrated in other districts because of politicization of aid; they want to help war-affected populations only or are directed to certain areas by the government." (Head of a CBO, Sri Lanka)

In most conversations, people noted the disappearance of aid or funds. Although people were careful to avoid terms like "corruption," many explained that aid did not reach them and that they could not explain what happened to the aid they were promised and, more directly, that they believed the providers, be they government or other agencies, kept a good portion of the funds. (Listening Project Report, Cambodia)

Endemic, Unchangeable, Understandable

“Corruption is institutionalized in Mali. It is just the way things are done. Some people are angry and frustrated about this situation, but some of us just expect it. Even if all of the aid does not arrive here and some gets taken out along the way, at least we do not lose all of it.”

- Villager, Mali

Although people express concern, even anger, at the corruption in their societies, many seem to accept it as inevitable. Some simply say they feel powerless to change it and doubt that anyone could do so. Others, however, note it is simply a part of their culture and systems and that these, overall, function well enough most of the time. That is, they express a kind of resignation that corruption is just one fact of life. A good number of people explain why corruption occurs and some also express understanding and sympathy for those who practice it. For example, when civil servants are un-paid or underpaid, some feel that they deserve to use their positions to "pay themselves." People are perfectly clear about what constitutes corruption—there is no ambiguity about that—but they nonetheless accept it as inevitable or understandable.

"Corruption is in place but at least something is happening. The development work does create jobs." (Hindu priest, Sri Lanka)

Some people in Kenya seem to accept corruption as the norm, citing numerous examples of unfinished projects or assets, such as vehicles that were given to groups only to be taken by the leaders when the project was finished and the donors stopped checking.... People talked about corruption and lack of accountability as a top-down problem, saying that impunity is culturally ingrained, especially given the weak legal system. Many seem to agree with the sentiment that it is acceptable to "eat" from where you work. (Listening Project Report, Kenya)

Angolan civil servants spoke frankly about the problems they face in trying to deliver adequate social services to the poor. Many are either not paid at all or are paid far less than a living wage. This, coupled with the low risk of being held accountable for breaking the law, provides a strong economic incentive for corruption and graft.
(Listening Project Report, Angola)

"I approached a donor to complain about beneficiary selection and was told privately [by local authorities] to put this in the past, so that they could continue to receive funding in the future from donors."
(Local man, Bosnia-Herzegovina)

Although people expressed anger about corruption, the majority felt powerless to change what they felt was the norm. Some felt they did not know how to protest, while others simply felt the systems that support corruption are too powerful to challenge and be changed. There was also a sense that those who are corrupt have impunity.
(Listening Project Report, Cambodia)

No Follow-Up, No Effective Accountability

Many people say that some aid-provider practices are, themselves, corrupt or at least have "corrupting" influences. They observe a widespread failure by international actors to monitor the processes and results of their aid programs. To distribute funds, and demonstrate little concern for what happens with them, is seen by many people as a form of corruption because the funding is often wasted and not leading to positive changes. They interpret this as a desire by aid agencies to be seen to be operational so they can continue to receive funding, without being accountable for actual outcomes.

Many, many, people suggested that agencies must do much greater follow-up on the activities they fund and undertake. Not to do so, they say, allows the theft, diversion, and other misuse of resources that they see repeatedly. Many go farther, saying that effective follow-up is important for more than "policing" corruption. It would, in addition, show concern for outcomes (which most see as missing now), and it would convey the message that outsiders are committed to working closely with the people who are on the receiving end of assistance to affect genuine progress. One large aspect of the failure to follow-up—which was, in some instances, equated with corruption—was the fact that the absence of donor agencies on the ground means that, when projects fail and have bad effects, aid recipients cannot hold these agencies accountable.

> 66 Some international NGOs receive huge sums of money, but we can never track the funds. They are not always accountable to villages and to the state. 99
>
> - Villager, Mali

Many people describe how easy it is to fake numbers in reports, and even to fake receipts. This ease, they say, facilitates and even encourages theft and diversion. Many conclude that if donors make it this easy to cheat, they must not really care. They say that the message conveyed by reporting procedures that are so easily bypassed or faked is that donors care more about getting the reports written with the "right" attachments than about what actually happens in the field in terms of either processes or outcomes.

The openness with which people describe these occurrences to Listening Teams suggests that these practices are widely known and somehow accepted as "normal" operating procedures. It also shows that current auditing and reporting procedures are quite often ineffective in achieving fiscal accountability.

Many people were frustrated with the lack of transparency and how little verifying, monitoring, and follow-up takes place, once projects get underway and after they are completed. A number of people mentioned that aid agency staff should be more present to increase transparency and to improve the flow of information. A Member of Parliament said, "We hear about hundreds of millions of dollars, but no office of accountability to see how the money is spent." (Listening Project Report, Afghanistan)

One community leader in Angola suggested that people who make charitable contributions to aid agencies are not given the full picture of what becomes of their donations. He said, with others nodding in agreement, that people in the U.S. who think they are helping the suffering need to know things are not done as they should be. He mentioned aid being stored in warehouses and sold in markets rather than being distributed equally.... His explanation was quite detailed and supported by his personal experience as a distribution truck driver for one international aid agency. (Listening Project Report, Angola)

A number of people in Bosnia suggested that there should be more and better monitoring of projects and of the NGOs and contractors who implement them, and that there should be more transparency and local reporting on where the money has gone and the impacts that agencies think they have achieved. A number of people said there was a lack of control over international assistance, that money was not spent properly and that a lot of resources had been misused. As one person noted, "It is easy to get a receipt for anything." (Listening Project Report, Bosnia-Herzegovina)

All Listening Team members in Cambodia heard suggestions about which entities aid should be delivered through to maximize impact and reduce corruption. Aid recipients continuously emphasized the need for more donor presence, more monitoring, and more conditionality on aid. (Listening Project Report, Cambodia)

> In Mali, people acknowledged that false, invented, or exaggerated numbers can easily be included in progress reports to the donors. For example, one person learned of a literacy program that a local NGO was running where several women had dropped out after the first class but reports to the donor kept stating high participation levels so that the organization would not lose the funding. Similarly, the owner of a private transport company that received several contracts from international agencies to transport commodities for food-for-work schemes told another Listening Team about many instances that he was aware of when village leaders falsified beneficiary lists so that they and their families and friends could benefit. (Listening Project Report, Mali)
>
> "I had a scholarship from a project, and I was close to individuals who managed resources. The students were told to come to the city ... even though there was money for paying them the bus fare, they were never paid. They were asked to sign blank vouchers." (Aid worker, Ecuador)

Even Worse, International Tolerance, Complicity: Missed Opportunities

Many say that international aid agencies have a prime opportunity to help communities change endemic systems of corruption because of the leverage they enjoy as providers of large amounts of support and funding. People often talk about how they had expected international agencies to help them break out of corrupt patterns and say that they see the aid providers' failure to monitor funds and outcomes as a missed opportunity to reduce corruption. As such, it represents at least tolerance of the misuse of aid's resources and, at worst, complicity in this kind of corruption.

Even those who explain that local leaders have little freedom *not* to honor systems of patronage, nepotism, and favoritism note that international agencies can provide the "excuse" that these leaders need to follow fairer distributional criteria. Knowing that the donor agencies will follow up can provide a rationale and support for people within the society who are under pressure to allocate resources according to traditional, endemic (corrupt) ways. They can "explain" to their constituents why they are "unable" to divert funds in these traditional patterns because, if they do, aid providers will hold them accountable.

Because the funding provided internationally is so large, this apparent tolerance of corruption is seen as, itself, worsening the problem (when it could have reversed it). Some are amazed at the failure of internationals to take up this opportunity; others are angered by it. In Aceh, for example, people were widely disappointed that international NGOs had not challenged the systems of nepotism and corruption when they provided assistance following the tsunami in 2004. Many people saw this failure as a missed opportunity.

"Corruption is ingrained in our culture. Internationals cannot change that. Kosovars must take responsibility. We must make sure we have the right incentives not to be corrupt. The transition will be difficult because the laws can be confused... more oversight from the international community would help the problem." (Community member, Kosovo)

"Internationals give money to the municipality to give to another NGO. With this process, the possibility is there to take some money." (Elderly man, Kosovo)

Whereas people rarely felt that NGOs were involved in corrupt or unfair practices, they were often disillusioned by what they saw as NGO tolerance of it, or at least reluctance to take steps to combat it.... There is no budget for lawsuits. (Listening Project Report, Bolivia)

While people acknowledged the local culture of corruption that has existed in Kenya for many years, they also suggested that donors have played a role in perpetuating it. They cited the lack of monitoring and verification of report and proposals, as well as the lack of presence on the ground and infrequent visits as playing a role in corruption within the aid system. Several people suggested that donors want to see their money spent quickly and that they do not seem to care about making real progress or reducing poverty or reducing corruption. "Donors played a role in allowing corruption because they were not using committees and were not involved inside of programs. They left individuals to control resources." (Church leader and others, Kenya)

While the government, local NGOs, and village leaders were all noted as possible misusers of funds, the UN, INGOs, and outside donors were also blamed for not ensuring that more resources reach people in communities. (Listening Project Report, Timor-Leste)

Misuse and Extravagance

High salaries, expensive housing and cars, fringe benefits, and ostentatious consumption by expatriates and consultants working in poor areas are seen by many recipients as unfair and wasteful. If funds are meant to help poor people, they say, then why do international staff spend and receive so much of it? Similarly, when local aid agency staff appear to enjoy luxuries that others cannot afford, people feel that international aid agencies pay those who work for them in overly lavish and unfair ways. Many also comment on the wastefulness of using expensive hotels for conferences and workshops when simpler and less expensive venues are available.

People are especially troubled by what they see as overspending when gains by intended beneficiaries fall short of expectations. This also is perceived as corrupt diversion of international aid from its intended use.

> " It is wasteful spending money on luxury living and not on Cambodian people. Money spent on per diems or cars and salaries could help so many Cambodian children.... They are cheating—the money does not go to the children—it's a kind of corruption.... They say the money goes to the country, but the [international organization staff] got $2,000 per month and $200 per diem and child care and car, etc. I want the international organization to show their overhead costs. "
>
> - Head of a local NGO, Cambodia

Some people concentrate on the lavish spending of international staff. Others say that this over-spending occurs more among local staff of international agencies. Though they differ on who benefits more, many perceive that aid benefits the providers more than those who should receive it and that this is, in essence, misuse of funding.

> "Corruption is on such a large scale here. A staff member of an international or local NGO, after a few years, is able to build a house worth 30–40 million CFA francs. Is that proportional to his income? There is not an NGO director in town without a personal vehicle, a nice house, a big boubou (a fancy and expensive outfit), and a beautiful woman!"
> (Male shopkeeper, Mali)
>
> "A lot of money that comes to the municipality is being diverted into private pockets. People in the municipality have a low salary, but build big villas." (School principal, Lebanon)

> The Listening Team members in Mindanao wondered whether, when the bulk of the aid goes to pay the high salaries for foreign consultants, and not to the intended recipients, if this was not also a form of corruption. (Listening Project Report, Philippines)

> "All I see are people coming in with big cars ... the only thing is talking, meetings, and rumors of an NGO holding functions. So where does the money go?" (Hotel guard, Kenya)

> A number of people expressed dismay that those who work for international and local NGOs often do so with ulterior motives. A school employee said that "Certain people want a luxurious life, form an NGO and get funding." One person responded to our questions about cumulative impacts with this disapproving assessment: "No outcomes, but a good lifestyle for local NGOs." (Listening Project Report, Sri Lanka)

Too Much Aid, Sometimes Too Fast

> " Donors pump a lot of money but it goes to individual pockets. Many organizations are registering to milk from donors in the guise of helping the community. Donors should not give large amounts like before—they share responsibility for making sure funds are spent well. Committees have sticky hands. "
>
> — A local Chief, Kenya

Another way people on the receiving end feel that aid providers feed into corruption is the timing of deliveries. Many see a link between the urgency to spend down project funds and opportunities for theft and diversion. Local actors, as well as some international staff, describe situations where the abuse and misuse of aid resources resulted from providers pushing too much aid into communities too fast. When sizable resources come into otherwise poor communities with the message that these must be spent quickly to comply with donor guidelines, it is not surprising that this prompts abuse. A number of people are surprised that international aid providers continue to make this mistake, which leads, they say, to misuse.

> Many local people were perplexed about the process by which aid flows into Afghanistan and into their communities, and why donors push to disburse funds quickly to meet external deadlines. In Kabul, people knowledgeable about the aid system expressed frustration with donors who often change funding structures and rules to spend money more quickly. People insisted that when the process is sped up, it creates opportunities for the money to be stolen. Officials in one ministry provided an example of just how this donor pressure to spend quickly undermines policies meant to reduce corruption and to build community capacity and ownership. Normally, funds go to the communities in three installments, and each disbursement has to be spent before the next one arrives. The first portion comes from the communities, and they have to raise the funds, put them into an account, and only then is the funding from donors added. However, one bilateral donor providing funds to the program insisted that the full amount be provided to the villages at one time. The program staff expressed concerns that the money could be stolen if given in this way. However, the donor insisted that their fiscal year was ending and that the partners had to spend the money quickly. They did as the donors demanded, and the money was gone. (Listening Project Report, Afghanistan)

Implications for International Assistance Going Forward

People in aid-recipient societies see corruption as important. Although it is impossible to know from their accounts whether corruption is, in quantifiable terms, marginal or significant, we do know that a great many people in a wide range of circumstances conclude that the corruption they observe and experience subverts the processes and purposes of international assistance. This reality poses three direct challenges to current policies and procedures of the international assistance community.

The first challenge is the evidence that the current policies, procedures, and systems that are meant to prevent corruption are not working. If so many people in so many settings recount experiences of theft and diversion and talk about how easy it is to hide them, then clearly new approaches are needed.

The second challenge arises from what people include in their definitions of corruption and of corrupting influences. The many comments about corruption expand the definition in ways that go beyond the definitions international donors and aid agencies use. People include what they perceive as "misuse" of resources by international actors themselves in the forms of "lavish" lifestyles, high salaries and consultant fees, and "waste" on ill-thought-out efforts. They include things not done to prevent abuse, such as when providers fail to follow up on projects to see what really happens and fail to support local people to overcome traditional systems of favoritism. And they include international actors' lack of accountability for failures and mistakes when projects do not achieve announced goals or, worse, fail. The fact that people broaden the discussion of corruption to include these actions and inactions of international aid providers is the second challenge to current aid policies and procedures that are intended to limit it.

The third challenge is in the messages conveyed by how people perceive international actors to deal with, or not deal with, corruption. Recipients' commentary on these messages relates to their analyses of the cumulative impacts of international assistance. When aid providers announce anti-corruption policies and enact procedures to track the use of resources, people say they welcome this. But, when these policies and procedures are not matched by on-the-ground engagement and follow-through, skepticism sets in. When recipients observe that providers seem to care more about distributing funds or writing a report to meet a donor schedule than determining that the funds can be absorbed without misuse or ensuring that program results are achieved, they take away the message that "anti-corruption" is only a slogan but not really an important practice.

What People Say Should Be Done

People in recipient societies make two suggestions about how aid providers can help curtail—or eliminate—corruption.

First, they urge international aid providers to be more "present." Listening Teams heard this theme everywhere. Many people say that if more aid agency staff are on the ground more frequently where aid is given, this presence could provide support to local leaders who want to break traditional favoritism patterns. It would reduce the easy falsification of both financial and narrative reports, and it would demonstrate that providers really do care about results. Most important, people say, more presence would enable the providers of assistance to develop healthier relationships with aid recipients, and these relationships, in turn, would support trust and respect, both of which are—according to many people—at the heart of the kind of colleagueship that would make aid more accountable and effective.

Second, people ask to be better informed about aid resources and efforts. (See more on this in Chapter 9) If people know how much aid has been provided and they can see how it is allocated, they say that they, themselves, will be able to reduce misuse and increase accountability. Working as a team of both providers and recipients to track the allocation and use of aid is, they suggest, a surer way of reducing waste and diversion than creating more protocols and procedures.

Conclusion

In the delivery system approach, donors have adopted strict anti-corruption policies and developed procedures meant to ensure that aid is not misused. For the most part, these policies and protocols come from the headquarters of aid providers, which are, themselves, accountable to taxpayers and legislators (in the case of government donors) or to foundations, private donors, and governments, in the case of international NGOs and other operational agencies.

To ensure full accounting for the monies, goods, and services provided, donors hire evaluators, accountants, and auditors to track funds and processes. Much of this tracking is focused on countering theft, diversion, or other misuse along each point in the delivery chain. Donor agencies want and expect (require) their partners and communities to work with them to prevent corruption, but the policies and procedures they rely on have been developed from the top down. People on the receiving side of international assistance emphasize that they must be actively engaged in decisions about aid to improve accountability. Without this involvement, corruption will continue and aid's effectiveness will, as a consequence, suffer.

● ● ● ● ● ● ● ● ● ●

CHAPTER NINE

INFORMING AND COMMUNICATING: NECESSARY BUT NOT SUFFICIENT

... in which we look at the roles of information and communication in international assistance and analyze how addressing the communication gaps can contribute to more effective and efficient assistance.

"If we only knew what the plans are, if we only knew how they decide, if we only knew when they plan to leave, etc.," aid recipients say.

"If we would just explain what we are doing and why," aid providers say.

"It's a communication problem," both say.

Aid providers and aid recipients recognize the gap in understanding that comes from inadequate information sharing and communication. Both feel that closing this gap—improving the flow and quality of information between providers and recipients—could correct many of the problems they face in providing and receiving international assistance. But is this true? Is a communication gap at the heart of the international assistance problems we have heard about?

The International Context

In recent years, global campaigns have emerged to encourage greater international aid transparency, and advocates have developed standards and protocols to ensure greater openness and information sharing by aid providers. In the humanitarian community, efforts are underway to ensure that even information is seen as aid.[11] Some donors now publish data on what they fund, and increasingly, governmental donors require funding applicants to agree to transparency protocols and report on their systems for ensuring that their activities and expenditures are available for public scrutiny. International aid agencies are providing more and more information to the people in recipient societies with whom they work in an effort to improve their accountability to their funders and to the people they support in aid-recipient countries.

---

[11] These include initiatives such as Publish What You Fund, International Aid Transparency Initiative (IATI), infoasaid, and Humanitarian Accountability Partnership (HAP), among others.

Improving transparency and information sharing fits very much within the delivery system approach of international assistance. Aid providers commit themselves to delivering more accurate information about more things. Even as the information they "share" may be responsive to recipient requests, the decisions about what to share and how to do so reside primarily with the providers. The policies and procedures for transparency and accountability are largely based on top-down initiatives and decisions. The forums where standards are set and protocols are written occur mostly in donor countries, though some include people from recipient countries. And procedures are, alas, increasingly complicated and structured, limiting adaptations to contextual differences. As these become required sections of project proposals and reports, there is the danger discussed previously that the focus of efforts to improve communication will shift from engaging more effectively with recipient communities to meeting donor requirements for transparency.

What People in Recipient Societies Say

66 The Listening Teams heard a lot about communication—not just participation in decisions, but simple respect. For example, answering communications; informing people about what was going on and what was expected to happen; assuring that a broad spectrum of people were informed, not just leaders; speaking to people as social equals; listening as well as speaking; and so forth. 99

- Listening Project Report, Bolivia

Even as these commitments take hold and providers enact transparency procedures, many people on the receiving side of assistance say they still feel uninformed and do not know how to find out what they want to know.

People see an information gap at every phase of international assistance, from the reasoning behind chosen program priorities, strategies, and geographical regions, to early community assessments, through implementation processes, up to the completion of an effort and the departure of the aid-providing organization. They name three areas that they care about the most: recipient selection criteria, project objectives and timeframes, and funding information. They want to know enough to feel involved in assistance processes. When they are not informed, they feel sidelined and are left with questions, suspicions, and disappointed expectations.

Beyond facts, people also want to *understand* why providers make the choices they make. People also want to offer their own ideas, feel that they are listened to, and know that their analyses are weighed in programmatic strategies and decisions. They want both better information and better *communication*.

Communication is *not* the same as information. Information deals with facts and explanations. It occurs in words, spoken or written. Communication occurs both verbally and nonverbally. Messages are conveyed explicitly and implicitly. Information can be delivered. Communication is a two-way process, involving the deliverer and the receiver in a continual feedback loop. The distinction has significant implications for international assistance. We return to this below.

"There are 150 NGOs in Bamiyan, but we don't know what they do."
(Faculty member of Bamiyan University, Afghanistan)

"There are a lot of NGOs around and they have big signs, but we don't have any idea what they do!" (Villagers, Mali)

"How can beneficiaries be linked with international donors? There is a lack of information by beneficiaries on what has been given out and what they ought to receive." (Staff of a local NGO, Kenya)

"Take the trouble to explain to people what your organization is doing. Most people will understand and you can avoid misunderstandings."
(Buddhist monk and leader of an NGO, Sri Lanka)

The Information People Want

1. Selection Criteria

The issue people in recipient societies most frequently raise is their lack of information about why providers select some individuals or groups for assistance and not others. As we have seen, the criteria for targeting often seem wrong to people where the assistance is given and, when they are not clear about who the providers include and why, they say that intergroup tensions often rise. This is true for both the people who "get on the list" and receive assistance and those who do not.

> 66 We don't understand the beneficiary selection process or criteria. The way our granddaughter was selected was by luck.... There has never been a public meeting to talk about everyone's situation and discuss aid and criteria. 99
> - Two grandparents raising their orphaned grandchildren, Zimbabwe

2. Project Goals and Timeframes

Many people say that they are aware of international aid coming into their communities, but they do not know either the agencies' activities or the intended impacts of the programs being implemented there. Many want to know the rationale behind assistance. Without this information, they say they cannot get involved in or support the assistance activities. Some say that when they do not know the facts, they imagine the worst.

> " For sure, international aid has done much good, especially in terms of infrastructure and training the people, but we don't know what its goals are because they don't speak to us clearly. That's why we imagine negative things. "
>
> - Former Provincial Councilor, Ecuador

People feel especially strongly that they should be informed about aid agencies' plans for ending project activities and leaving their areas. When they are not informed about the timing or conditions of a project's ending, some feel abandoned. Most say that this information would enable them to plan ahead and handle the departure with less disruption to their lives.

"Why are some individuals and households selected in our village and others are not?" (Group of villagers, Ethiopia)

"We don't have enough income, capacity, and power to change our situation. We don't know where to go. We don't know why some people are being helped in Sri Lanka and others are not."
(Displaced survivors of a mudslide, Sri Lanka)

A large number of people in Aceh expressed their dismay that they did not have enough information about aid and aid processes. "I do not want to blame anyone; I just want information," said one man as he commented on problems with aid distributions. Others said, "If we understand, then we can be patient." "The process of receiving aid is not clear to beneficiaries." "How aid works is confusing."
(Listening Project Report, Aceh, Indonesia)

"I don't understand for what period of time they have come."
(Villager, Bolivia)

"Exit and phase out strategies need to be discussed with local government and other relevant organizations from the start. It should be part of the capacity building process for local government units to plan for sustainability." (A local NGO program director, Philippines)

"One mistake that we have noticed is the closure of the aid [programs] leading to depression on the part of those who were benefiting from them. If, in the course of delivering the aid, there had been awareness-raising as to the fact that the aid was only temporary, would only be there to help them for a little while, they [the beneficiaries] would have understood this and the [closing of the programs] would not be cause for such sorrow." (Government official, Angola)

"If funding will be discontinued, donors should inform you early so you can plan for it. Otherwise the people are upset. Organizations should have an exit strategy and give one year's notice." (A Palestinian NGO director, Lebanon)

In several areas in Ethiopia, people were confused about the lifespan of projects initiated by NGOs. In one village, non-beneficiaries expressed confident hopes about receiving livestock from a project; however, the NGO is no longer working there. (Listening Project Report, Ethiopia)

3. Funding Allocations

❝ International agencies can give information to the people and tell the whole village so all the people will have the information about the projects and budget. When so many people know the project, no one can manipulate it or do corruption. The information is open to everyone. ❞

- A woman, Timor-Leste

People want to know more about aid resources. They want to know how much money is involved, where it goes, who gets it, and what is accomplished with it. Many say they hear on the radio or television about millions of dollars of international assistance entering their country, but they do not know where it goes and do not see its impacts. Without clear information about funding, people often suspect corruption and diversion. When people's expectations exceed what they see as results, questions about the use of funds become even more urgent.

"Villagers, INGOs, and donors should all know how much money is spent on things in the village. They bring projects into our village and we should know where the balance goes." (Commune Council Members, Cambodia)

"Problems in the community persist despite the assistance because of how the work is done. No one knows how much money is given and what it is used for." (A local Chief in a Nairobi slum, Kenya)

"Awareness about international aid should be shared equally among the rural populace. For example, we hear about funds for a cattle project only after all the funds have been used." (Education officer, Solomon Islands)

"There are times when we don't know the balance remaining in the project budget." (Political official, Ecuador)

"I find that aid that is given to Mali lacks transparency. The population is not informed at all. They say that Mali has received X amount of CFA francs but the population never knows how this assistance is used. The population only hears that on the radio, but as to how the aid will actually be spent is not revealed." (Director of a primary school, Mali)

"There has been a sense of discomfort amongst the population in recent years. We regularly hear on the radio and television and read in the newspapers, that important amounts of assistance have been given to Mali. Communications go no further than these simple announcements. There is no explanation for how and where funds will be used. For the average citizen, they naturally wonder, 'where has all this money gone?'"
(Senior level government official, Mali)

What Happens to Information: Why People Do Not Know

Most aid agencies try to inform people about their activities and feel that they are doing so effectively. Yet, people in recipient countries feel they "don't know" many things. How does this happen? People in recipient societies cite three reasons.

1. Simply no effort is expended.

People say that some assistance providers simply do not invest the time or effort to share information.

> "Some advisors don't want to share knowledge. They just sit in front of computers, writing reports. Some [advisors] just do it for themselves and when their contracts are over, they never come back."
>
> - Ministry official, Timor-Leste

2. The wrong people get the information.

Donor and NGO staff may believe they have effectively informed a community by meeting with a village chief or other local representatives, but people in these communities often report that those who were in the meeting do not share the information discussed with the wider community. In some cases, the people who are consulted are not seen as legitimate representatives. In other places, specific groups, such as women or youth, are not included in any consultation processes.

Within communities, other information bottlenecks exist. Information given to one family member—often the male heads of household—may or may not be transmitted to other family members as aid agencies expect. The timing of a community meeting or consultation may also be inconvenient for some people.

> ❝ When a project is financed, the content has to be disseminated among all the people of the community or sector, not only among the leaders. Sometimes the people know nothing of the project; it's the leaders that have all the information. This is not correct and lends itself to manipulation and the improper use of the funds. ❞
>
> - An indigenous community leader, Ecuador

People feel that aid providers should try to understand existing community structures or mores that limit information flows. Where information goes and how it is used can determine whether an aid effort is effective. People in recipient areas make the point that aid agency staff must talk with (and listen to) a broad range of community members to ensure that information reaches everyone who is integral to an aid effort and that their involvement is encouraged. People also emphasize the importance of "going off the main road" to reach people who are more remote and outside the usual communication channels.

"The communication center does not work. They communicate with us only when they have an interest in doing so."
(Leaders of a women's organization, Bolivia)

Implementing agencies said they are stuck in the middle—that donors may not want the information (i.e., on staff salaries) to be revealed and that doing so could create suspicions. Others said that they do not believe that communities have a right to know such detailed information and that it can lead to even greater suspicions and misunderstandings.
(Listening Project Report, Kenya)

Listening Teams noted that some donors do not allow international agencies to tell people (or the government) how much is to be spent on projects, while others favor greater transparency. Some NGO staff mentioned that displaying the monetary values of their projects has led to people complaining that other groups or areas get more than their group, or that the posted amount was not spent there, causing tensions. Many agencies therefore do not publish financial information on projects. (Listening Project Report, Bosnia-Herzegovina)

"When they consult with just a few people, the community thinks they are only visiting—they don't feel it is a consultation. Sometimes the NGOs don't give the real perspective that they are there to do a consultation... then it results in projects in the community." (Refugee, Thai-Burma border)

"The *kebele* (village chief) selects men to go talk and get told things. They don't come here. They don't ask women. It's far away, and because women are busy, they can't go to meetings. Nobody comes here." "I don't go to meetings because my husband doesn't allow me and he doesn't tell me what goes on there." "The woreda and *kebele* [local jurisdiction] leaders make most of the decisions about projects but there are no women in leadership positions." (Women, Ethiopia)

"They will not understand if the explanation is done only once. People from the village need to have things explained many times. For them, seeing is believing; thus, the need to prove to them."
(Villagers, Myanmar/Burma)

"[Villagers] not only don't know, they don't ask, they aren't told. Sometimes they know something, sometimes they don't. They've got too much to think about. They learn from their parents they are not supposed to ask a question. It's part of the Cambodian culture—if you ask too many questions, you are a bad boy."
(Local staff of an international organization, Cambodia)

"They show up only rarely, sometimes late in the day, and only talk to certain old men of the village." (Group of women, Angola)

> Some international NGO staff in Aceh, in an attempt to be "culturally sensitive" in an Islamic society, assumed that male staff workers could not speak directly to women. However, Listening Teams found that, for the most part, women were very willing to speak to men, and both local and international staff who know Aceh well point out that, possibly compared to other Islamic cultures, there is a very high level of openness between men and women in public in Aceh. If women do not feel comfortable talking with a man, they express this very directly. In general, such public conversations are quite acceptable and accepted.
>
> (Listening Project Report, Indonesia)

3. The wrong approach is taken.

Aid recipients also describe differences in communication styles and cultural practices that inhibit effective information sharing and communication between providers and recipients. For instance, some cultures deem it rude to question information in public. In such cases, aid providers may be misled into assuming that people have the information they need and are content with what they know. In some places, people express disagreements gently and quietly, so foreign aid providers, who are accustomed to more direct discussion, may miss or misread their true feelings. When notices are placed on bulletin boards, people who cannot read (or who cannot read the language in which the notices are posted) do not get the information. And, sometimes, international staff may be overly cautious about cultural sensitivity and miss opportunities to talk with certain groups.

> " It is a good idea to learn how the people in each culture view themselves—do they see themselves as strong, weak, positive, sad, do they value humor, do they value talking about their ideas, or do they feel it is rude to talk about their ideas? "
> - A Karen elder, Thai-Burma border

What Does Good Information Do?

People say that when they feel informed, they feel respected and are able to participate more effectively. Credible information made widely available reduces the opportunity for rumors to spread and be believed. It allows people to plan ahead and integrate aid provider inputs into their own lives and plans. In some areas, people reported that they had seen important improvements in information sharing and consultation, but that much more needs to be done.

" It is important that local people understand the project. If they do not understand well, the project will not be successful. "
- Men, Myanmar/Burma

Improved accountability is one of the most frequently discussed outcomes of improved information sharing. Many people note that they need full information to hold aid providers and their partners accountable for where the money goes. They also note that knowing what aid agencies claim to be doing for them in their proposals, reports, and publicity would enable them—the receivers—to hold these donors accountable when they do not fulfill their claims.

" NGOs should provide information on how much has been funded and which specific areas and programs. Accountability within NGOs is lacking. Who are they responsible for and who do they account to? There is no known information on exactly how much comes to the various communities and the agency's office. Nobody knows how much is available in the community, so it is difficult to hold the NGOs accountable. "
- Local NGO staff person, Kenya

"The needs identification came from us." (Community leader, Bolivia)

"At first, the work of the international agencies was not transparent and clear. It created problems between all the people who want the money. Over the last five years, there have been a lot of improvements…. Now the aid agencies are transparent in the implementation and in the way they spend the money. International aid supported local organizations in improving their management qualities. This made the projects more organized, and more accounting on the performance and implementation is given." (A school principal, Kosovo)

The Listening Team in Cambodia discussed how communication with recipients, trust building, and NGO and donor presence all contribute to an environment in which the recipient of aid has the knowledge, confidence and outside support to do their part to fight the lack of transparency and to improve accountability. (Listening Project Report, Cambodia)

"We don't want support for money and reporting only. We like organizations that keep in touch, that send emails and information."
(Palestinian NGO Director, Lebanon)

Beyond Information: Communication

Improved information sharing clearly could go a long way toward closing the communications gap both aid providers and recipients identify. It enables people to do more forward planning, follow the money and hold people accountable for its use, and ensure that those who are eligible for assistance receive it, resulting in a fairer distribution of aid resources. The very act of informing people about plans, decisions, funds, and goals signals respect for them. As we have seen, people on the receiving side of assistance see an important linkage between having information and improving the impacts of international assistance.

Beyond the facts they want to know, recipients also want better *communication*. They want to have ongoing, two-way, respectful conversations between aid providers and aid receivers.

Many who complain about problems with international assistance—unwanted items, unsustainable projects, corruption, disrespect for local culture, misguided priorities, unfair distribution—also say that providers could avoid these mistakes through "better communication." Aid providers not only need to give aid receivers more and better information, they need also to listen to the feedback, thoughts, criticisms, and ideas of recipient communities. Aid receivers also want responses to their feedback, and hope for thoughtful, ongoing conversations.

Implicit Communication

Further, as was clear in discussion of the intangible long-term impacts of assistance (Chapter 3), aid-delivery processes also communicate implicit messages. How providers set assistance priorities, announce policies, enforce procedures and evaluate results also send implicit messages to (but not from) aid recipients. When donors write policies that condemn corruption and enact procedures to prevent it, but do not follow up in the field to ensure that funds are in fact spent as intended, the words communicate one thing while the actions (or lack of actions) communicate another. When donor agencies announce their respect for recipients but do not provide sufficient time in the planning process to hear and respond to the ideas of people who receive the aid, their actions belie the words.

Aid providers also convey implicit messages by how they comport themselves. When they listen attentively and indicate that they have heard what recipients have said, they send one signal. When they look at their watches repeatedly and appear to be in a hurry, when they look at the notes they are writing more than at the person giving information, when they neither adjust a program in response to ideas from the receiving community nor explain why not, these actions send a message of disrespect.

Conclusion

Transparency and information sharing go a long way toward closing the communication gap between aid providers and aid-receiving communities. In addition, as aid providers share more facts and improve recipients' understanding of their intentions and work, they also, as we have said, convey the implicit message of respect. This respect is critical for the longer-term relationships that so many people in recipient societies say are central to effective, accountable assistance.

Every interaction of aid providers and recipients adds dimensions of communication to the assistance process. Projects and programs that aim to improve communication need to move beyond standards and procedures for delivering more and more accurate information to embrace this wider scope of communication. They need to address not only the exchange of ideas through words, but also the exchange of messages through actions. Good communication is critical to positive relationships, and more importantly, to effective assistance.

A Coda: Necessary But Not Sufficient

Transparency, broad information sharing, and continual two-way communication are necessary, but they are *not* sufficient, to correct all of the problems with international assistance people in aid-recipient societies report. Information and communication are important components of effective assistance and are of central importance in the relationships that are developed between aid providers and aid recipients. But, they do not ensure that actions change.

Aid providers and aid recipients need not only to listen to and respect each other, but also to be willing to change what they do and how they do it based on what they hear. Sometimes, even though they are fully informed and understand a program and its rationale, people on the receiving end of assistance may nonetheless think that it is wrong. They may disagree with its premise, its intent, its content, or its processes. Knowledge and understanding do not automatically lead to agreement.

The American nineteenth-century philosopher, Henry David Thoreau, once said, "The question is not what you look at, but what you see." Paraphrasing his point, we might say here that the question is not what you listen to, but what you hear. This idea captures the importance of effective communication strategies in international assistance. However, beyond this, the question is not just what we hear, but what we do about it. This moves us past improving communications to additional and necessary steps to improve actions.

• • • • • • • • • •

CHAPTER TEN

OBSTACLES TO MEANINGFUL ENGAGEMENT

… in which we hear from providers of assistance who are eager to engage with people in aid-recipient countries about challenges that they face in trying to meaningfully involve them.

> " Donors need to be honest and forthright about what they really mean by 'participation.' Is it simply a consultation with communities to get approval or support for a project that has already been pre-determined, or really to decide jointly and to work together? "
>
> - Aid worker, Senegal

> " What I like about our donor is that they like to learn from us. They say they learn a lot from our seminars and our process. In order to do that, they spend time with us and participate in these discussions. A donor is a true partner if they are listening to us. If they listen and learn they will accompany you and won't dictate. We share an understanding: we are in this together. A lot more is possible then. "
>
> - Director of a local NGO, Philippines

The participation of local people in processes and projects that aim to support positive and lasting changes in their lives is widely recognized as an important principle in international assistance. The engagement of aid recipients is both a means and an end to effective assistance. It is expected to lead to greater recipient ownership and accountability, as well as sustainability of results. One can trace the expansion and evolution of participatory approaches in the last few decades by looking at the vast amount of literature, manuals, and frameworks produced by the international assistance community. As one aid worker exclaimed, "We are swamped in participation!"

Chapter 6 reviewed how the principle of participation has too often been inflexibly "proceduralized" within the approaches of aid agencies. After "participating" in many assessments, meetings, and activities planned by aid providers, recipients often say they are disillusioned. In virtually every conversation, they ask what these supposedly "participatory" approaches have achieved. They see little evidence that their involvement shapes decisions or actions. They say that most externally initiated participatory processes fall short of what they, as aid recipients, would consider meaningful and constructive engagement.

So, why is genuine participation so difficult to achieve? In this chapter, we look at the challenges from the point of view of dedicated aid providers. They truly want to engage with the people on the receiving side of assistance, and they express their frustration about the barriers and bottlenecks in the current delivery system approach to aid that limit their ability to do so.

Obstacles Aid Providers Face in Engaging Aid Recipients in Meaningful Ways

1. Engagement requires time.

Experienced donors and aid agency staff report numerous challenges in building relationships and effectively engaging people in aid-recipient societies. One of the most prevalent and frustrating is the pressure they feel to do things quickly. They acknowledge that they sometimes ask local partners and community members to participate in hurried consultative processes that are "more for form than substance." As noted earlier, aid workers say that much of their time is consumed by writing proposals and reports. They complain that they spend the time they want and need to hold meaningful and in-depth conversations with people about local priorities and existing capacities in meeting these agency-driven deadlines. An aid worker in Senegal admitted, "It is true that an obstacle to getting real involvement of local populations may be the cost and time commitment that it entails. With the emphasis on speed and efficiency, there is little time for true community involvement." Aid agency staff in headquarters and the field say that their agencies place greater priority on satisfying donor requirements than on engaging effectively with people in recipient communities.

> 66 What the people need is time to talk and to express themselves. And NGO staff do not have the time. Talking to the villagers is more important than giving them stuff. 99
> - Local NGO staff, Myanmar/Burma

Constraints of rigid timeframes and reporting obligations are more common than not among aid-providing agencies, and many recognize that these are incompatible with the expectations and realities of people in recipient communities. Furthermore, aid providers say that reporting formats seldom require them to elaborate on the substance and quality of their relationships with local people and organizations.

They say that their agencies are focused on speed of delivery rather than on the time it takes to build relationships with recipient communities.

"If we are going to listen, donors need to have longer timeframes, and to accept higher overheads from NGOs." (Aid worker, Australia)

"Not until I spent three weeks staying in a village did I feel like I was getting truthful information about what the community really needed and wanted. Only after they knew me and trusted me, did this frank exchange became possible." (Aid worker, Lebanon)

"We wish we could go out more to visit communities and spend quality time with people, but administrative requirements don't allow us to go out as much as we would like to. It's also expensive."
(Feedback Workshop participant, Mali)

"We talk about 'participation' but it is always the donor which makes the final decisions because it has the money." (Aid worker, Senegal)

"The understanding of donors is still small. [With greater presence] donors could give better information, and improve people's lives. And they could build good relationships. Presence is important. The donor must adapt to the community and be invited in, if not, they can't be received/accepted. They need to adjust well to each community.... And they can't assume that everyone is the same." (Local aid worker, Timor-Leste)

"Presence takes time and money. Presence requires openness and humility. Presence involves prioritizing time and resources and delineating roles and responsibilities between levels (outsider, insider, stakeholders of various sorts)." (International Aid Worker, Denmark)

"Those donors who have been on the ground longer understand the local dynamics and political context better. But people get moved around like ambassadors and that knowledge often goes with them. For example, people rarely ask, 'Where is the source of authority and credibility within this community?' before they enter one. In some places, it does not reside with the local government, but rather perhaps in the local rebel group or community leader. Knowing local context is important in order to bring even more change through a development process. But this takes time." (City official, Philippines)

2. Engagement requires access and presence.

Aid providers say that they can be constrained in their efforts to ensure recipients' participation by a lack of access. Sometimes this is limited by their agencies' concerns about security (real or perceived). Some communities are hard to reach, off the main roadways, and in remote locations. Some are inaccessible for other reasons (again, real or perceived), as when traditions in a society restrict women to their compounds. Finally, community perceptions of an aid agency's politics or agendas may mean that local people do not want to have anything to do with the staff of that agency.

Many aid agency staff reflect on how their lack of access restricts their ability to develop an accurate, unfiltered picture of community capacities and needs, and to foster respectful relationships with local people. For example, aid workers in Iraq (based in Jordan for security reasons) note that their inability to work in project locations and their resultant inability to accurately assess the situation and social climate have resulted in confusion and a lack of consensus about how to address problems. When insecurity restricts access, aid-providing agencies lack an understanding of the context, which in turn affects how they prioritize and conduct their work, thus limiting the effectiveness of their assistance.

> 66 When a community is not engaged, the problem is more than just lack of sustainability. These projects are more easily destroyed by violence. 99
>
> - Aid worker, Afghanistan

Some aid agencies working in insecure places feel they must keep their identity as an aid organization hidden. This further limits their ability to build trust and develop relationships with local people. Being able to engage people by jointly discussing issues, prioritizing, and making decisions together becomes a remote goal for organizations that do not have regular opportunities for talking with and listening to people on the ground.

3. Engagement requires resources.

Aid providers describe two resource constraints on engagement. First, it costs money for their agencies to ensure that staff have the time and means to live in or travel to remote places. Sufficient vehicles and fuel are necessary for not just one visit, but multiple, repeated visits. Providers need to be able to stay long enough to listen and respond so that recipient communities become truly engaged. Though many donors talk about the importance of local participation and ownership, some simply do not invest the resources needed to truly enable it.

At the same time, engagement requires the time and effort of recipient communities, and these are often in short supply, too, particularly in areas where people are poor. To address this constraint, some aid organizations pay for people to participate in project activities, such as trainings or meetings, by covering costs of transportation and food or by compensating them for their time. However, both recipients and providers have a range of opinions on this practice and its effects. Disagreements and differences of experience reflect variations in the long-term effects of this practice on aid-receiving societies and a range of opinions about the quality of engagement that payments actually prompt.

Many practitioners observe that such payments can undermine the principle of participation, influence the quality of relationships, raise expectations, and create perverse incentives for people to "participate" in aid processes. Some aid providers and recipients believe that paying people to participate erodes the traditions of mutual self-help in communities. Others argue that aid agencies should not expect local people to contribute their time, input, and efforts without being compensated. Some feel that giving people money or other forms of payment constitutes a gesture of appreciation and respect for people's effort to spend a day away from their regular duties. Others feel that payments for involvement feed into a monetization of what should be community-based or volunteer activities.

When external aid providers pay people in recipient communities to "participate" in activities, this payment can also inadvertently undermine the ability of local organizations to engage people effectively. Local organizations report that when wealthier aid providers pay higher participation fees, recipients will sometimes refuse to engage in activities that do not pay as well. Local NGOs can rarely compete with international agencies' larger budgets and find it challenging to work with the "professional workshop-goers" that this precedent has created.

> 66 When an Iraqi sees an international NGO, he sees money. We are a local NGO, so we cannot provide a lot and try to work with communities to express the importance of participating. 99
> - Local aid worker, Jordan

Aid providers, government officials, and local organizations raise concerns about two negative long-term effects of paying for participation. First is that it is unsustainable and fosters dependency. Second, aid providers observe that some people use these stipends as a source of income and often are participating for their own benefit rather than to support positive changes in their communities. When this occurs, aid providers doubt that payments really buy meaningful participation.

"Some community people are very experienced with outside projects, and it is good. They demand more information and they know what is useful and what is not. They ask for information on the donors and the implementers. But it is true; training is a difficult issue here. In some communities, if an NGO provides training the community asks for money for coffee-breaks and lunches and also for the per diem. But when they talk about it later they say it was not interesting and useful." (Aid worker, Tajikistan)

"If we cover transport and lunch, people would come to our meeting. First it was passive participation, but then little by little, the participation began to be more active ... we did not promise much and people provided useful information." (Feedback Workshop participant, Jordan)

"Communities identify the word 'project' with money. To collaborate, they must be paid, and if they are not paid, this will become an issue because they will be waiting for money. We also need to change the mentality of people so that it is better for the future. The project is this: we give this contribution; the community has a separate contribution."
(International aid worker, Timor-Leste)

"Currently the system uses projects [that are] identified with money; to accept a project there must be money. People are not being educated. This is not valued. The orientation has shifted to business."
(Local aid worker, Timor-Leste)

"Some payment to ensure their participation helps to make the project successful, but how far do we take this? People start working with NGOs for money. The UN pays big money, and we cannot afford to pay that."
(International aid worker, Jordan)

4. Engaging people effectively requires specific skills.

Aid providers need to know how to listen, how to facilitate problem solving, and how to manage conflict if they are to be effective in engaging people in recipient communities. Some aid workers tell of experiences where they tried to engage village and community-based development committees in jointly drafting development plans. They describe how the process was immensely complicated because many disagreements arose about what needed to be done, how, when, and by whom. They admit that they and their partners are often not equipped with the skills needed to handle such disagreements. Many are more comfortable promoting "passive participation" in carefully orchestrated meetings with select local leaders than in facilitating "active participation" that engages a broad range of people in deep and sustained processes. As a result, aid providers can skew consultative processes in ways that actually limit participation.

> 66 Listening is a special skill and you cannot assume everyone can do it appropriately in all contexts. It needs to be nurtured instead of assumed. This has implications on training and on the need for awareness of how our way of listening is based on our assumptions about the world and our way of working. 99
>
> - Aid worker, Australia

Many aid providers recognize that they need to know more about the areas where they work. Again, this requires that their donors and their agencies value time spent in listening, learning, discovering, and analyzing the contexts where they provide assistance. To nurture genuinely collaborative approaches to planning and decision-making requires people with skills and a real interest in the people, and the politics, of recipient countries. Aid-providing agencies and their staff must approach their work with a range of colleagues broadly and inclusively—and, more importantly, with humility and a real commitment to sharing decision-making power.

"Participation doesn't always work; it depends on the person facilitating it, on the attitude of the facilitator. When we present ourselves to the community as arrogant, and we think we are the one that knows everything, sometimes it creates reluctance on the part of the community. An attitude of a person can be translated by the community as an attitude of the NGO. So if it's a good attitude, this symbolizes that it's a good NGO. If it's bad, it's a bad NGO." (Aid worker, Timor-Leste)

"It's always important to, at least with a rapid exploration, go to the community and explore with the community. If you rely on community leaders, you could be relying on gatekeepers that aren't true representatives of the community." (Government representative, Colombia)

"Influential people sense they are losing power when [community] participation increases. The power relations in the community are important to take into consideration when involving people. This means that the process is more complicated and you need more time." (Aid worker, Afghanistan)

> **"With community participation, how do we know what's working? In Soviet times, [Communist] Party people visited the *kolkhoz* (collective farms) and everyone looked busy working and participating. Now it is the president or the new political party people, or in many cases INGO visitors who come to visit and everything looks fine on a short visit."**
> (Aid worker, Tajikistan)
>
> **"There is a lack of genuine participation in projects. The 'list of participants' doesn't actually represent a genuine participatory process."**
> (Staff of the Ministry of Culture, Colombia)
>
> **"Sometimes it is difficult to motivate the community to participate in needs assessments since many people are not interested in a program that they feel will not help them."** (Aid worker, Lebanon)

5. Engagement needs to be measured and valued.

Many of the dimensions of engagement—the quality of relationships, levels of trust, equity in decision-making, ownership—are not easy to measure. The ways that aid agencies typically measure participation focus primarily on the number of meetings held, the number of people who attend, the diversity of "stakeholders" present, or the number of projects community groups implement. These, most aid providers say, do not provide effective assessments of the value or quality of participatory processes.

In Listening Exercises and Feedback Workshops, aid recipients and providers alike talked about the need to measure quality rather than quantity. They note that just because something is measurable does not mean it is what should be assessed. An aid worker in Australia asked, "If 10 years ago we had more solidarity but couldn't show the results, was it because we couldn't figure out how to measure it? How do local people see the changes?" A practitioner in London concurred, suggesting, "We need to say 'yes to mess' and see that logframes are too narrow to measure many of the changes we seek to support."

When the focus of evaluations is on quantitative measures, the incentives for aid providers follow. They plan more community meetings or other events where they can count heads to demonstrate engagement. Aid workers in Geneva talked about how aid providers need to change the definitions of what is "real work" with what is "important work" and discussed how aid agencies could likely get better donor support if they could define and measure "engagement" with more rigor and precision.

The ways that aid providers evaluate their staff, partners, programs, and overall impacts need to include assessments of how effectively they engage with a broad range of people—and to what end. Rewards and penalties should reflect the value that aid agencies say they put on ensuring meaningful participation of people in recipient societies. Many aid agency staff suggest that the skills they need to engage local people effectively—such as language skills, cultural sensitivity, and a collaborative approach—need to be valued in recruiting, included in competency frameworks, and assessed in staff evaluations. As one long-time aid worker admitted, "We are being rewarded for our talking rather than our listening."

> **" It's a carrot but where's the stick? The stick isn't there because you're probably not going to be fired if you're getting your funding, reaching goals, but not getting relationships right. "**
> - International aid worker, London

Aid workers recognize that local people need to feel that the time they spend together actually adds value to the aid process and to see the results of their participation in the outcomes. When local people do not feel that they have a real "voice" in decisions—as described earlier when recipients discussed prepackaged programs and the predominance of outside agendas—it is understandable that they will not want to waste any more time and effort in so-called participatory processes.

Evidence from aid providers, as well as aid recipients, demonstrates that when people feel that they have a voice and have been listened to, they can accept outcomes they may not, themselves, have suggested. They will trust a system that creates plans based on real discussions and their real involvement in making decisions that affect their lives. Many aid recipients say that they are open to different approaches from those that they suggest, noting that, "we can understand your constraints if you just explain them to us."

• • • • • • • • • •

CHAPTER ELEVEN

CONCLUSION: ACTING ON WHAT WE HAVE HEARD

The Evidence Prompts Change

"International assistance is a good thing." So said many, many people who live in countries that receive such aid. The idea that people and countries with relative wealth are willing to help those with less makes the world a better place than it would be without this commitment. But, most recipients and many providers say, the *system* of international assistance is deeply flawed. The lasting benefits are too often disappointing. Many intangible cumulative impacts (dependency, increased intergroup tensions, distrust, and disrespect) are negative. The waste of resources is immense. The enterprise is, they tell us, not doing the good it is meant to do.

The Starting Point

People want *not to need* international assistance. They want to live politically, socially, environmentally, and economically secure lives without depending on outside help. What they want, therefore, from international assistance is a *system* that supports indigenous processes so that outside aid will be unnecessary.

The current approach of international assistance does not accomplish this.

What, Specifically, Is Wrong?

The detailed evidence this book reports can be summarized in two essential points.

First, the organization of international assistance as a delivery system through which some people "provide" while others "receive" is inimical to its stated objectives and undermines the very principles on which it is based. People who live in recipient societies say that this system turns them into "objects" of others' decision-making and planning, rather than engaging them as subjects in their society's progress. They note that a system that is organized to deliver focuses on gaps and needs to be filled, rather than on existing capacities and structures that should be reinforced. Aid structures and functions that are designed to facilitate delivery inevitably become supply-driven, and the resultant top-down direction of goods and services violates the principles of participation, ownership, and sustainability essential for effective aid. Externally-driven deliveries are an inadequate mechanism for promoting positive change in the recipient societies.[12]

Second, no universal blueprint exists for creating peace or promoting humanitarianism, good governance, or development. Standard policies and procedures and pre-packaged programs the international assistance system offers do not adequately reflect differences in the contexts where aid is provided. People on the receiving side say that effective assistance must take account of contextual differences within and across their areas. They note that standardized approaches and models that come from outside can limit (and even obviate) recipient community creativity.

Toward a New Paradigm?

Many aid providers and aid recipients agree that the international assistance system needs to change fundamentally. Tinkering at the edges will not address their critiques. One more donor policy, one more carefully elaborated procedure, one more training program, one more conference of donor and recipient countries will not ipso facto correct the problems they identify.

Many feel that it is time for a new international aid paradigm.

A paradigm is an approach—a way of doing things—that is accompanied by a set of beliefs or assumptions, held by a majority of the people involved in the field where the paradigm prevails. It is more than just an accepted theory; it entails an entire worldview.[13] When such a paradigm encounters repeated "anomalies" (again, Thomas Kuhn), people within the field begin to question it, to look for ways either to explain and incorporate these or to find alternative ways of addressing them. When the challenges to the prevailing thought are significant and numerous enough, and enough people are seeking alternatives, this prompts the discovery or invention of a new paradigm. Paradigm shifts do not just somehow happen. They grow out of experience and are accomplished by people inside the system who look for a better way of understanding and/or accomplishing something.

---

[12] Equally, internally driven processes in recipient countries can be mired in tradition and habit, geared toward maintenance of status quo power and wealth relationships, and trapped by inadequate resources. We have noted that, if societies knew how to achieve their own development, justice, and peace, they would do so without recourse to international assistance.

[13] Thomas S. Kuhn, *The Structure of Scientific Revolutions,* (Chicago: University of Chicago Press, 1962).

" The phrase 'paradigm shift' is scary for many people. It calls into question everything they are doing and they think they have to start from scratch, relearn everything, and all their hard won experience is irrelevant. In fact, it is precisely the hard-won experience that prompts the shift. No paradigm shift is possible without people experimenting around the edges of a system to see if they can shore up the sections that are collapsing. It is these experiments that show the way toward the new paradigm. It is these experiments that need to be brought from the edges to the center of the profession. In other words, every reader knows enough to start the paradigm shift today. "

- International program director, USA

How Different Is What People Want from What We Have Now?

What people want is an international assistance system that integrates the resources and experiences of outsiders with the assets and capacities of insiders to develop contextually appropriate strategies for pursuing positive change. The idea of international assistance needs to be redefined away from a system for delivering things and reinvented to support collaborative planning. Real help (as opposed to delivery of resources) would involve mutual insider/outsider analysis of the context, generation of options, and shared decisions about the best strategy for pursuing the desired changes.

The difference between this and the delivery system may sound subtle, but it is in fact a difference of night and day. The delivery system starts from the fact that donors are there to provide things. The alternative starts from what people have, not what they need; it identifies what they already know and do well, not the gaps in their knowledge and skills. Pre-planned projects and standardized procedures imply that there is a model that if properly imported will bring change. A broad analysis of context and exploration of options sends the message that there are many potential paths toward positive change and that international assistance exists to help people explore possibilities and choose from among them the one(s) that will most directly accomplish their priorities. Knowing they have options can reinforce, or in some cases unleash, recipient communities' sense of efficacy.

ELEMENTS OF TWO PARADIGMS: A COMPARISON

Externally Driven Aid Delivery System	Collaborative Aid System
Local people seen as beneficiaries and aid recipients	Local people seen as colleagues and drivers of their own development
Focus on identifying needs	Focus on supporting/reinforcing capacities and identifying local priorities
Pre-planned/pre-determined programs	Context-relevant programs developed jointly by recipient communities and aid providers
Provider-driven decision-making	Collaborative decision-making
Focus on spending on a pre-determined schedule	Fit money and timing to strategy and realities on the ground
Staff evaluated and rewarded for managing projects on time and on budget	Staff evaluated and rewarded for quality of relationships and results that recipients say make lasting positive changes in their lives
Monitoring and evaluation by providers on project spending and delivery of planned assistance	Monitoring, evaluation, and follow-up by providers and recipients on the results and long-term effects of assistance
Focus on growth	Planned draw down and mutually agreed exit/end of assistance strategy

The theory of change that lies behind such an alternative approach may be stated as follows: The role of international assistance in promoting positive social, political, and economic change in the countries where it is offered is to expand the range of options that people in that society can consider, to engage with them in weighing the costs and benefits of each option and, from this, to co-develop and co-implement a joint strategy for pursuing the changes they seek.

Sound Familiar?

The reader may be thinking, "But, we already do this." "This is not new." And the reader would be right!

Remember, a paradigm shift comes only after many people inside a system see problems with the prevailing paradigm, experiment with options, and find aspects of options that have superior results. Many of the efforts underway at the highest levels to reform current aid approaches are based in a broad, growing awareness of past inadequacies. Many aid providers are engaged in processes directed toward greater inclusion of recipient voices and ownership (from national governments to local communities). The Listening Project is just one of multiple efforts urging aid providers to move to a system that is more effective.

If this is the right direction for a new approach, then it *should* sound familiar.

Understanding the *idea* that international assistance should move from a supply-driven delivery approach to an alternative is not so hard. But, if the idea is clear, the *transformation of the system* to match the idea is not. Changing the complex and multi-layered system of international assistance is an enormous and challenging task. The day-to-day practices and the mechanisms that support aid must change, sometimes radically. Shifts in thinking must be accompanied by shifts in behaviors, for aid providers and, probably, also for aid recipients. How do we even begin to envision what steps to take? One way to do this is to consider which aspects of the aid system are "in reach"—what it is that providers can change at any time.

What Aid Providers Control

Policies, procedures, and resources are the three primary instruments of international assistance. Providers of aid articulate and promulgate their ideas, principles, and intentions through policies; they institutionalize predictable mechanisms for planning, implementing, and evaluating through procedures; and they allocate resources such as funds, goods, services, technical assistance, training, and expertise. Because providers develop these tools, providers can change them. As such, these tools are the instruments through which to realize any paradigmatic approach. Therefore, a paradigm shift will require, and will be realized through changes in, these three instruments.

Imagine reinventing policies, procedures, and resource allocations so that they encourage and support collaborative exploration of options, and contextually appropriate development of strategies. What might this look like?

Policy development and use. In the current system, donors and providers present policy statements and strategies as fixed points of departure for their subsequent programming and funding choices. In a collaborative approach, policies and strategies would be written in an exploratory fashion, raising an important issue, inviting the reflection and discussion of many people on both the providing and receiving sides of assistance and bringing together broad international learning with the perspectives, priorities, and experiences of recipient colleagues. The intent would be to move policy discussions and subsequent strategies forward on the basis of shared analysis and priority-setting. Even though policies may be tied to fixed, non-negotiable political positions, the *applications* of policies in different places would vary to fit those contexts without inadvertent negative impacts.

Procedures. Providers and recipients agree that international assistance should be based on clear standards of action that are predictable, transparent, and consistent. However, the procedures now in place are overly complicated and time-consuming and often do not accomplish their intended purposes. The collaborative approach would apply Occam's razor[14] to any procedure to ensure it is simple, clear (in multiple languages), and open to discussion and review to see if it works or not. Procedures would never become an end in themselves but always one (and only one) means toward an end. Insofar as they are the simplest, clearest, and most effective way to achieve a goal, they would be used. If other means were found to accomplish the same goal more effectively, simply, and clearly, the procedure could be circumvented and/or abandoned. Such flexibility would allow for adaptations to different contexts, based on feedback from people in those contexts about the usefulness and impacts of any procedure.

Allocation of resources. We have seen that the organization of the international assistance system around the delivery of external resources distorts both the relationships between aid providers and recipients and the processes employed through this system to promote positive change in recipient countries. In a collaborative approach, provision of external resources would be just one, and not necessarily the primary, mechanism for expanding the options under consideration by those involved in planning a change strategy.

Imagining an Alternative Funding System: An Illustration

Changes in how funding is provided are the most critical—and perhaps the most difficult to achieve—in moving from the delivery system to a more collaborative approach. To make these changes, legislatures, taxpayers, private donors, politicians, and diplomats will need to be convinced that the required flexibility does not abrogate responsible stewardship. Because this is such a thorny area, it provides an apt example of what kinds of changes are required and how difficult these will be.

Starting with the evidence provided by people in recipient societies, we know of four significant counterproductive effects of the current funding processes:

1. Funding procedures are increasingly time-consuming. Hours and days are spent applying for, reporting on and accounting for funds. And this diverts priority, attention, energy, and time from interactions between aid providers and recipients. Funding procedures need to be radically simplified. They need to be fit to purpose, in other words, to be clear, direct, honest, and manageable.

---

[14] Occam's razor asserts that the simplest solution is often the best. That is, all things being equal, simplicity should be favored over complexity.

2. Funding procedures now in use fail to stop corruption and, in a number of cases, the sheer quantity of funds and the schedule on which they must be spent (to meet donor requirements) inadvertently feed into systems of diversion, favoritism, nepotism, and politicization. (See Chapter 8 for a fuller discussion of how this corruption occurs.) Amounts of funding and procedures for managing it need to be contextualized.

3. Arrangements by which funding is available cause distortions in the relationships between aid providers and aid recipients by focusing on resource transfers from the former to the latter, rather than relying on existing recipient community capacities and the exploration of options to strengthen them. They undermine local contributions and ownership of aid processes.

4. Current funding procedures encourage waste. Just one example can be found in the many instances when the need to spend down funds by the end of a reporting period prompts unnecessary and repetitive conferences or workshops in expensive hotels, rather than ensuring that these funds are used throughout an activity to engage local people effectively. Procedures should allow for under-spending and reward it.

Creative funding approaches—such as pooling funds, creating accounts that communities can quickly and easily draw on, providing cash instead of goods, and creating consortia to reduce competition among operational agencies and encourage cooperation—have been used but often encounter institutional and political resistance. Undoing the existing funding system and creating an effective alternative will not be easy. But these efforts do demonstrate aspects of the experimental approach required for a paradigm shift.

Some principles should guide the development of an alternative funding system: "Enough, but not too much"; "Available, but not necessarily spent"; "Steady, but no burn-rate requirement"—such funding principles would connect resource flows to a mutually developed strategy and to a given context. Funding should follow the exploration of options rather than drive it. External monies should play a subsidiary role, supplementing local capacities and resources only as needed. The approach should reduce waste by more closely linking funding flows to events on the ground. It should reduce the time, energy, and attention that overly complicated procedures require. It should promote contextually appropriate, joint strategies for eliminating theft, mismanagement, and corruption.

The "Alternative Four Steps" below illustrate how funding procedures could involve recipient communities and, at the same time, be simplified. These four steps would clearly require the aid providers' hands-on involvement, but it is possible that this would require less time than staff now spend on managing, explaining, and reviewing complicated financial procedures.

Alternative Four Steps for Funding

Step One: Early Listening Funding. All providers would engage with and listen to a variety of people in a prospective recipient country or community before developing a proposal for funding. Any aid provider could draw on a pool of funds made available by individual, or consortia of donor agencies for this purpose. Funds would cover costs of an exploratory field visit and conversations with many people in and around the area (with a lot of listening) to identify local priorities and options for pursuing them that would benefit from external assistance. Incentives would encourage providers to work together to avoid misusing the time and effort of people on the receiving side.

Step Two: Proposal Development. Providers and a recipient group (identified as trusted by people in the proposed area) would together construct a funding proposal. No templates would be required. A proposal would be expected to tell as much as needed to make the case that the plan is a good one from the points of view of the recipient groups (as well as other groups nearby who will not be included in the activity but who will be aware of it and judging it). This could be lengthy or brief. The rule of thumb would be that proposals make the case, provide alternative scenarios of how the process of the work could/would likely unfold, define the time-span, and attach potential cost figures to these alternatives. Budgets would be based on an "up to but no more than" figure.

Step Three: Disbursement of Funds. Funds should be easily accessible as needed. No draw-down schedule should be set. Funds could be set aside in some form of "bank account" on which programmers (which should include recipients as well as providers) could draw as needed (providing brief explanatory notes to the donor at the time of each withdrawal). Aid providers and recipients would together monitor the disbursement and use of these funds and provide transparent information to all involved to reduce opportunities for corruption or mismanagement.

Step Four: Reporting/Accounting. The rule should be simplicity, clarity, and honesty. Donors, aid providers, and aid recipients should decide together on appropriate timing of reports, ways to assess effectiveness, and mechanisms of accounting prior to any agreement on funding. Reports should be made available publically, and recipient communities should not only contribute to them, but also review them.

Most people on the receiving side of assistance want accountability as much as the providers (and their donors, taxpayers, and legislatures) do. They, too, want to eliminate diversion, corruption, and waste. It should, therefore, be possible to develop contextually solid procedures for ensuring that material (and other) resources are reliably and honestly used—and that this assistance makes a positive difference. Under an alternative paradigm of aid, the international assistance community is challenged to identify funding and accounting approaches that are based in local context and that rely on existing cultural systems that force and maintain accountability.

Who Is Responsible for Change?

In some sense, no one is responsible for making the changes that are needed and, in another sense, everyone is. In some sense, no one is able to make these changes and, in another, everyone is.

Because the international assistance system is so large and layered, it can seem impossible for any part of it to change without all of it changing. But because it is, in fact, individual people who join, support, engage in, and perpetuate this system, it is also true that change by any individual can contribute to and possibly prompt the broader systemic change that is required. As nature demonstrates, the change of a large and complex system goes both ways. Systemic shifts, such as rainfall or climate changes, prompt changes in individual species' behaviors. And changes at the margin in the behavior of individual organisms (such as the fish that first climbed out of the water) can also ultimately lead to systemic change.

At every level, it is the people who are engaged in providing aid that are the key to systemic change. Anyone who participates in the system as it now is can, by changing how they participate, also change the system. There are as many ways and moments to change what is as there are moments in which we fit in and carry on with the current system. That is, paradigm shifts occur when people change the way they do things.

Policy-makers. Policy-makers are responsible for rethinking how they construct their policies. The brief discussion in Chapter 4 about the relative success of gender programming makes the point that policies regarding gender equality were broadly discussed among and across all societies. Advocates came from all societies (as did resisters!); resources were put into conferences, programs, and research to explore how best to achieve the goals; and enough time was spent on both policy development and follow through in programming to bring results. A closer look at these processes is suggestive of how other priorities may be broadly discussed and collaboratively turned into shared policies.

Procedure-alists. Everyone in the aid system who oversees, develops, or complies with procedures (which is everyone!) is responsible for changing them. Every agency could begin to make these changes by reviewing the time spent in complying with each standardized process in use. The review should also look at results. Any procedure that takes staff time away from engaging in the work with aid-recipient communities should be simplified. The new system will be working when aid providers and aid recipients spend the majority of their time and effort developing and pursuing their strategies for change, rather than on filling out forms and writing proposals or reports.

Funders. The people who work on the funding aspects of international assistance must take on the responsibility for generating new approaches. These approaches should be built on collaborative responsibility for tracking funds, have the flexibility to respond to changes in contexts, and simplify reporting and accounting procedures. Once these are generated, implementers must inform those who make policies or insist on certain procedures (such as legislative bodies) about problems observed under the current system and the options for correcting these. They must be adept at persuading taxpayers, lawmakers, and private donors that they can reduce both waste and corruption through their collaborative system (a case that is not difficult to make given the evidence!).

A Note about Staffing

Beyond policies, procedures, and the allocation of resources, aid providers control who they hire. They define what they consider critical attributes and credentials for staff; they set expectations about how staff should act; they establish priorities staff should pursue; and they train, reward, pay, and even punish staff. Every story of effective aid told by aid recipients included a description of particular staff who worked in ways that developed respect and trust with aid recipients. The connection that recipients make between lasting, positive aid outcomes and the characteristics of aid-agency personnel are striking. Taking time to talk and listen, getting to know people, understanding the community, developing a relationship of trust, following through on promises, showing concern for results, being "present"—all of these contribute, according to people who experience aid, to effective assistance. On the other side, doing research or experimenting with different approaches for their own career advancement, making lots of money, spending ostentatiously (especially in bars and restaurants and on housing), always being in their offices, always being in a hurry, and always working on their computers were cited as exemplars of ineffective staff behaviors.

> An aid worker sat in the breakfast room of the Geneva hotel typing on her computer between sips of coffee. She was at her agency's annual meeting during which headquarters staff and field partners from many countries could meet and get to know each other. An African colleague arrived at breakfast, greeted

the woman typing and asked if he could join her. She nodded yes and kept typing. He started to speak. She said, "Not yet. Just a minute," and kept typing. He sat, then tried again and got the same response. On the third try—"Not yet, in a minute," he got up and left. She did not look up. Fifteen minutes later, she gave a satisfied smile, closed her computer and got up to leave. Her report was done!

In the Listening Project's many Feedback Workshops where aid providers reflected on the ideas and analyses of recipient communities, the issue of aid-agency staffing came up again and again. Aid providers agree with recipients. The qualities they should recruit and train for are those that make a person good at relating to, engaging with, and listening to others. However, being a nice person is not enough. Effective international assistance also requires specific skills and knowledge.

Personnel departments of assistance-providing agencies have a special role in perpetuating the delivery system paradigm or in helping support a more collaborative shift. A place to start the shift would be by listening to and learning from counterparts in recipient societies. Many have experience with a variety of people, and many can connect staff competencies and performance with concrete outcomes.

Why Does Change Seem So Difficult?

Almost universally, the people who work in providing aid describe the limits of their influence on the system rather than their strategies to change it. Ironically, these same aid-providing agencies and their staff are committed to, and talk about, "empowering" the recipients of their aid to make systemic changes in their societies! What is wrong here?

"My agency would never let me spend that much time in the field," says the senior NGO manager who has just complained that he cannot know the real impacts of his agency's projects because of limited field time. "I have to convince my Parliament about the value of assistance," says the head of department in a major bilateral donor agency who has just admitted that he funds projects that claim they will make peace in a region in a three-year timeframe, even though he knows results would be better if monies were spent more slowly over a longer period. "I know that we are providing things that are not needed, but I have to keep the delivery on schedule in order to be ready to apply for the next tranche of funds," complains the agency field director.

These comments are not unusual, and they are telling. These people *are* their agencies. They are senior staff. They make policy, set standards, supervise others, determine their own schedules, and set their own and others' priorities. They are able, smart, and aware. They recognize that their work is flawed and that there are better ways to achieve their intended results. Yet, they feel compelled to keep the system going as it is. What they are saying is, "I have to do it wrong so I can keep money coming so I can do it wrong again to keep money coming…."

Why do responsible and conscientious individuals accept what they recognize as wrong-headed limitations on their ability to do good work? Why are they content to stay within the confines of a system that they acknowledge too often fails to achieve its goals?

What is going on here? Is this the best we can do? People in recipient societies think not. They think that fundamental change is not only needed—but it is possible.

Possibilities!

Every one of the moments described above represents an opportunity (a missed opportunity) for changing the system. It is impossible to exaggerate the importance of each of our choices about whether we will live within the structures and confines of the delivery system and, by doing so perpetuate it, or whether we will find and take opportunities in our spheres of action to make the changes that are needed. Every moment of business-as-usual is a lost moment for making change. Thomas Kuhn noted that in science, a paradigm shift takes time. People accustomed to one way of working are hard to convince. Many resist change where their particular expertise may be challenged. Historically in the scientific community, he notes, older scientists have to retire or die for younger scientists, who have been exposed to alternatives through their training, to take over and make the changes.

International assistance is peopled by self-designated change-agents. Aid providers devote their efforts to improve the life prospects of aid recipients through changing systems that marginalize and impoverish them. The question on the table now is: Can a field of change agents change itself?

A Final Word on Listening

As we end this exploration of what people say about international assistance, we should reiterate the importance of listening, itself. Time and again, after some lengthy critical conversation with a recipient group, someone would thank the Listening Team simply for asking these questions and paying attention to the answers. Many times, they commented on the uniqueness of this experience. Sadly, they said, it had never (or seldom) happened before!

If we did nothing else to improve the aid system, the very act of adding occasions and opportunities for aid providers to listen to people with whom we work, and to let them know that their ideas and judgments are valued, would by itself bring a fundamental shift in the relationship of aid providers with aid recipients. It would address the current of cynicism we hear and transform the sense of disrespect that lies at the heart of much of the disappointment with, and resentment of, aid's impacts. Listening is a value. As one of the quotations above says, we should "take a deep breath" in the midst of our reporting and funding deadlines. We should, in short, listen to what people say. To do so is fascinating; it is also helpful. And it is the responsible and respectful thing to do.

• • • • • • • • • •

Appendix 1

Listening Project Field Visits and Feedback Workshops

(in chronological order)

Listening Exercises

Aceh, Indonesia (November 2005)	Reports in English and Bahasa Indonesia
Gulf Coast, United States (June 2006)	Report in English
Bosnia-Herzegovina (July 2006)	Reports in English and Bosnian
Ethiopia (October 2006)	Reports in English, Amharic and Oromiffa
Angola (November 2006)	Reports in English and Portuguese
Bolivia (November 2006)	Reports in English and Spanish
Zimbabwe (December 2006)	Report in English
Thailand (March 2007)	Reports in English and Thai
Kosovo (July 2007)	Reports in English, Albanian and Serbian
Sri Lanka (October 2007)	Reports in English, Sinhala and Tamil
Kenya (October 2007)	Reports in English and Swahili
Cambodia (November 2007)	Reports in English and Khmer
Thai-Burma Border (November 2007)	Reports in English and Karen
Ecuador (March 2008)	Reports in English and Spanish
Timor-Leste (October 2008)	Reports in English and Tetum
Afghanistan (May 2009)	Report in English
Lebanon (July 2009)	Reports in English and Arabic
Mindanao, Philippines (August 2009)	Report in English
Solomon Islands (November 2009)	Report in English
Myanmar/Burma (December 2009)	Report in English
Mali (December 2009)	Reports in English and French

Feedback Workshops

Dushanbe, Tajikistan (2008)

Copenhagen, Denmark (2008)

Geneva, Switzerland (2008)

Dili, Timor-Leste (2008)

Washington, D.C., USA (2009)

Kabul, Afghanistan (2009)

Beirut, Lebanon (2009)

Amman, Jordan (2009)

Bonn, Germany (2009)

Bamako, Mali (2009)

Dakar, Senegal (2009)

Bogota, Colombia (2010)

London, England (2010)

Manila, Philippines (2010)

Melbourne, Australia (2011)

Canberra, Australia (2011)

Appendix 2

Organizations that Participated in the Listening Project

Organizations listed below are designated according to how they were involved in the Listening Project: Listening Exercise (LE), Feedback Workshop (FW), or Consultation (C), and by the countries where they participated.

Academy for Educational Development (AED) USA (FW)

Act for Peace-National Council of Churches in Australia Australia (FW)

Action Africa Help International (AAHI) Kenya (LE)

Action Aid Cambodia (LE)

Action Asia Myanmar/Burma (LE)

Action Couverture et Développement (ACD) Mali (LE)

Action Jeunesse et Environnement Senegal (FW)

Action Rechereche pour le Développement des Initiatives Locales (ARDIL) Mali (LE)

Active Learning Network for Accountability and Performance in Humanitarian Action (ALNAP) UK (FW), USA (C)

Adventist Development and Relief Agency (ADRA) Denmark (FW), Philippines (FW), Solomon Islands (LE)

Afghan Aid Afghanistan (LE, FW)

Afghanistan Institute of Rural Development (AIRD) Afghanistan (FW)

Afghanistan Ministry of Finance Afghanistan (FW)

Afghanistan Ministry of Rural Rehabilitation and Development (MRRD) Afghanistan (LE, FW)

Afghanistan National Development Strategy Working Group (ANDS) Afghanistan (FW)

African Office for Development and Cooperation (OFADEC) Senegal (FW)

Africare Mali (LE)

Aga Khan Trust for Culture (AKTC) Afghanistan (LE, FW)

Agence Evangélique de Développement du Mali (AEDM) Mali (LE)

Agency Coordinating Body for Afghan Relief (ACBAR) Afghanistan (FW)

Agency for Technical Cooperation and Development (ACTED) Afghanistan (LE), Jordan (FW)

Aide et Action Mali (LE, FW)

AidWatch Philippines Philippines (FW)

Alliance for Peacebuilding USA (FW)

American Friends Service Committee (AFSC) Cambodia (LE)

American Red Cross Thailand (LE), USA (FW)

American University of Beirut - Issam Fares Institute Lebanon (FW)

American University School of International Service - Center for Peacebuilding and Development USA (FW)

Anglican Church of Kenya - Christian Community Services and Directorate of Social Services Kenya (LE)

Appui à la Promotion des Aides Familiales et à L'enfance (APAFE) Muso Danbe Mali (FW)

The Asia Foundation Cambodia (LE), Timor-Leste (FW)

The Aspen Institute USA (FW)

Association Malienne pour la Survie du Sahel (AMSS) Mali (LE)

Australian Agency for International Development (AusAID) Australia (FW), Solomon Islands (LE), Timor- Leste (LE, FW), USA (C)

Australian Council for International Development (ACFID) Australia (FW)

Australian People for Health, Education and Development Abroad (APHEDA) Solomon Islands (LE)

Australian Red Cross Australia (FW)

Balay Mindanaw Foundation, Inc. (BMFI) Mindanao, Philippines (LE)

Bank for Agriculture and Agricultural Cooperatives (BAAC) Thailand (LE)

BBC World ServiceTrust UK (FW)

Bearing Point USA (FW)

Belun Timor-Leste (FW)

BRAC Afghanistan (FW)

British Embassy Lebanon (FW)

British Red Cross UK (FW)

Bureau d'Appui aux Collectivités Rurales (BACR) Mali (LE)

Cambodian Center for Human Rights (CCHR) Cambodia (LE)

Canadian International Development Agency (CIDA) Mali (LE, FW); Senegal (FW)

CARE Australia Australia (FW)

CARE International Afghanistan (FW), Angola (LE), Bolivia (LE), Ecuador (LE), Ethiopia (LE), Kosovo (LE), Mali (LE, FW), Switzerland (FW), Tajikistan (FW), USA (C), Zimbabwe (LE)

CARE UK Philippines (FW), UK (FW)

Caritas Mali - Commission de Pastorale Sociale Mali (LE)

Caritas Sénégal - Sécours Catholique Senegal (FW)

Caritas Tajikistan Tajikistan (FW)

Catholic Fund for Overseas Development (CAFOD) Timor-Leste (FW)

Catholic Relief Services (CRS) Afghanistan (LE), Angola (LE), Bolivia (LE), Bosnia-Herzegovina (LE), Ecuador (LE), Ethiopia (LE), Kosovo (LE), Lebanon (LE), Mali (LE, FW), Mindanao, Philippines (LE), Philippines (FW), Timor-Leste (LE, FW), USA (FW, C), Zimbabwe (LE)

Cellule d'Appui aux Initiatives de Développement - Mali (CAID) Mali (LE)

Center for Peace and Conflict Studies (CPCS) Myanmar/Burma (LE)

Center for the Support of Native Lands USA (FW, C)

Centre for International Studies and Cooperation (CECI) Mali (FW)

Centro de Multiservicios Educativos (CEMSE) Bolivia (LE)

CHF International Bosnia-Herzegovina (LE), Ethiopia (LE), USA (C)

Christian Aid UK (FW)

Christian Children's Fund Ecuador (LE), USA (FW)

Christian Ecumenical Action in Sudan (CEAS) Kenya (LE)

Church World Service USA (FW)

Colombian Ministry of Culture Colombia (FW)

Community and Family Services International (CFSI) Philippines (FW)

Concern Afghanistan (LE)

Consortium of Bangsamoro Civil Society (CBCS) Mindanao, Philippines (LE)

Consortium of British Humanitarian Agencies (CBHA) UK (FW)

Consortium of Humanitarian Agencies (CHA) Sri Lanka (LE)

Coordination of Humanitarian Assistance (CHA) Afghanistan (FW)

Dakahumas Kenya (LE)

DanChurchAid Denmark (FW)

Danish Association for International Cooperation Denmark (FW)

Danish Hunters' Association Denmark (FW)

The Danish Mission Council Denmark (FW)

Danish Red Cross Denmark (FW)

Danish Refugee Council Kosovo (LE)

Department for International Development (DfID) Tajikistan (FW)

Department of Social Welfare and Development, Philippines (DSWD) Philippines (FW)

Deutsche Gesellschaft für Internationale Zusammenarbeit (GIZ) Colombia (FW), Germany (FW), Timor-Leste (LE, FW)

Development Alternatives Inc. (DAI) USA (FW)

Development Initiatives UK (FW)

Development Partners in Action (DPA) Cambodia (LE)

Development Workshop (DW Angola) Angola (LE)

Disaster Tracking Recovery Assistance Center (D-TRAC) Thailand (LE)

Ecosystems Work for Essential Benefits, Inc. (ECOWEB) Mindanao, Philippines (LE)

Emergency Capacity Building Project (ECB) UK (FW)

The Esquel Group USA (FW)

Eurasia Foundation Tajikistan (FW)

Evaluar Consultores Colombia (FW)

Éveil Mali (LE)

Family Action UK (FW)

Feinstein International Center, Tufts University USA (C)

The Fletcher School of Law and Diplomacy, Tufts University USA (C)

Fondation Stromme Mali (LE, FW)

Food and Agriculture Organization of the United Nations (FAO) Afghanistan (FW)

FORUT Sri Lanka (LE)

The Fritz Institute USA (C, FW)

Fundación Caminos de Identidad (Fucai) Colombia (FW)

Fundación para los Comunidades Colombianas (FUNCOL) Colombia (FW)

Fundación Synergia Colombia (FW)

Gazton Z. Ortigas Peace Center
Philippines (FW)

Geneva Peacebuilding Platform,
Geneva Centre for Security Policy
(GCSP) Switzerland (FW)

Georgetown University - School of
Foreign Service USA (FW)

German Development Service (DED)
Germany (FW)

German Federal Ministry for
Economic Cooperation and
Development (BMZ) Germany (FW)

Groupe de Recherche d'Etude de
Formation Femme-Action (GREFFA)
Mali (LE)

Groupe de Recherche et d'Appui pour
les Initiatives des Populations (GRAIP)
Mali (LE)

Groupement des Artisans ruraux
d'Intadeyné (GARI) Mali (LE)

Haburas Moris Timor-Leste (FW)

Helen Keller International (HKI)
Cambodia (LE)

Helvetas Mali (LE, FW), Switzerland (FW)

Humanitarian Accountability
Partnership (HAP) Switzerland (FW)

Humanitarian Futures Programme UK
(FW)

IBIS Education for Development
Denmark (FW)

IBON Foundation Philippines (FW)

Impact on Health Kenya (LE)

Initiatives for International Dialogue
(IID) Mindanao, Philippines (LE)

Institute for State Effectiveness USA
(FW)

InterAction USA (FW, C)

International Aid Services Denmark
Denmark (FW)

International Center for Not-for-Profit
Law (ICNL) Tajikistan (FW)

International Center for Peace in
Mindanaw (ICPeace) Mindanao,
Philippines (LE)

International Committee of the Red
Cross (ICRC) Jordan (FW)

International Federation of Red
Cross and Red Crescent Societies
(IFRC) Aceh, Indonesia (LE), Thailand (LE),
Switzerland (FW), USA (C)

International Labor Organization
(ILO) Lebanon (FW)

International Medical Corps (IMC)
Jordan (FW)

International Organization for
Migration (IOM) Jordan (FW)

International Orthodox Christian
Charities (IOCC) Bosnia-Herzegovina (LE)

International Rescue Committee (IRC)
Aceh, Indonesia (LE), Ethiopia (LE), Jordan
(FW), UK (FW), USA (FW, C)

Interpeace Switzerland (FW)

Irish Red Cross Sri Lanka (LE)

Joint Aid Management (JAM) Kenya
(LE)

Kalimudan Mindanao, Philippines (LE)

Karen Development Network
Myanmar/Burma (LE)

Karen Educational Department Thai-
Burma Border (LE)

Karen Human Rights Group Thai-
Burma Border (LE)

Karen Women's Organization Thai-
Burma Border (LE)

Karen Youth Organization Thai-Burma
Border (LE)

Karuna Myanmar Social Services
(KMSS) Myanmar/Burma (LE)

Katilingbanong Pamahandi sa Mindanaw Foundation, Inc. (KPMFI) Mindanao, Philippines (LE)

Kindernothilfe (KNH) Ecuador (LE)

Konrad Adenauer Stiftung (KAS) Kenya (LE)

Lasallian Justice & Peace Commission Philippines (FW)

Lebanese Economic Association (LEA) Lebanon (FW)

Life & Peace Institute USA (C)

Local Capacity for Peace International (LCPI) Kenya (LE)

Luta Hamutuk Timor-Leste (FW)

Lutheran World Federation (LWF) Kenya (LE)

Mathare Youth Talented Organization (MYTO) Kenya (LE)

Médecins du Monde (MdM) Jordan (FW)

Médecins Sans Frontières Holland (MSF-H) Jordan (FW)

Médecins Sans Frontières Suisse (MSF-S) Switzerland (FW)

Mercy Corps Aceh, Indonesia (LE), Afghanistan (FW), Bosnia-Herzegovina (LE), Ethiopia (LE), Kosovo (LE), Lebanon (LE), Sri Lanka (LE), Tajikistan (FW), UK (FW), USA (FW, C), Zimbabwe (LE)

Mercy Hands Jordan (FW)

Mindanao Commission on Women (MCW) Mindanao, Philippines (LE)

Mindanao Peoples Caucus (MPC) Mindanao, Philippines (LE)

MISEREOR Germany (FW)

Misión de Apoyo al Proceso de Paz en Colombia de la Organización de los Estados Americanos (MAPP/OAS Mission) Colombia (FW)

Mission East Tajikistan (FW)

Movimiento por la Paz el Desarme y la Libertad (MPDL) Kosovo (LE)

MVH Consult Denmark (FW)

Nabaa (Development Action without Borders) Lebanon (LE)

Nagdilaab Foundation Mindanao, Philippines (LE)

The Nature Conservancy USA (FW)

Norwegian Agency for Development Cooperation (NORAD) USA (C)

Norwegian Church Aid (NCA) Mali (LE, FW)

Norwegian Ecumenical Peace Platform USA (C)

Nyein/Shalom Foundation of Myanmar Myanmar/Burma (LE)

Observatorio de la Cooperación al Desarrollo en el Ecuador Ecuador (LE)

Office of the Presidential Advisor on the Peace Process (OPAPP) Philippines (FW)

Open Society Institute (Soros) Tajikistan (FW)

Operation Mercy Tajikistan (FW)

Organization for Economic Co-operation and Development (OECD) USA (C)

Overseas Development Institute (ODI) USA (C)

Oxfam America Cambodia (LE), Ethiopia (LE), Sri Lanka (LE), Senegal (FW), USA (FW, C), Zimbabwe (LE)

Oxfam Australia Australia (FW), Solomon Islands (LE)

Oxfam GB Mali (LE, FW), Sri Lanka (LE)

Oxfam International UK (FW)

Partner Microcredit Organization Bosnia-Herzegovina (LE)

Partners Kosova Kosovo (LE)

Peace and Justice (Swe Thaha) Myanmar/Burma (LE)

Peace Tree Network (PTN) Kenya (LE)

PeaceBuilders Community, Inc. (PBCI) Mindanao, Philippines (LE)

People in Aid UK (FW)

People in Need Jordan (FW)

Plan International Ecuador (LE), Philippines (FW), Thailand (LE), Timor-Leste (FW)

Pour un Sourire d'Enfant (PSE) Cambodia (LE)

Premiere Urgence (PU) Jordan (FW)

Programa de Coordinación en Salud Integral (PROCOSI) Bolivia (LE)

Public Committee for Promotion of Development Tajikistan (FW)

QuestScope Jordan Jordan (FW)

Raks Thai Thailand (LE)

Reach International Healthcare and Training Mindanao, Philippines (LE)

Regional Development Agency (REZ) Bosnia-Herzegovina (LE)

Rehabilitation and Research Centre for Torture Victims Denmark (FW)

La Rencontre Africaine pour la Défense des Droits de l'Homme (RADDHO) Senegal (FW)

Research Triangle Institute International (RTI) USA (FW)

Rotary International Denmark (FW)

Sanayee Development Organization (SDO) Afghanistan (LE, FW)

Save the Children Australia Solomon Islands (LE)

Save the Children Denmark Denmark (FW)

Save the Children Sweden Lebanon (LE, FW)

Save the Children UK UK (FW)

Save the Children US Bolivia (LE), Ethiopia (LE), Tajikistan (FW), USA (FW, C)

Security Research & Information Centre (SRIC) Kenya (LE)

Seeds of Peace Africa International (SOPA) Kenya (LE)

Sewalanka Foundation Sri Lanka (LE)

SEXSALUD Bolivia (LE)

Shuhada Organization Afghanistan (LE, FW)

Silsilah Dialogue Movement Mindanao, Philippines (LE)

Single Parents and Widowers Support Network (SPWSNET) Zimbabwe (LE)

Solomon Islands Red Cross Solomon Islands (LE)

South East Mission (SEM) Myanmar/ Burma (LE)

Southern Christian College (SCC) Mindanao, Philippines (LE)

Spectrum Myanmar/Burma (LE)

State University of New York at Buffalo USA (C)

Stop Sahel Mali (LE)

Support for Tropical Initiatives for Poverty Alleviation (STIPA) Kenya (LE)

Swedish International Development Cooperation Agency (Sida) Mali (LE, FW)

Swiss Agency for Development and Cooperation (SDC) Tajikistan (FW)

Taipei Overseas Peace Service (TOPS) Thai-Burma Border (LE)

Tak Border Child Assistance Foundation (TBCAF) Thai-Burma Border (LE)

Tematisk Forum Denmark (FW)

Terre des Hommes Jordan (TDH) Jordan (FW)

Thai Red Cross Thailand (LE)

Thingaha Gender Working Group Myanmar/Burma (LE)

Le Tonus Mali (LE)

United Nations Children's Fund (UNICEF) Afghanistan (FW)

United Nations Development Program (UNDP) Afghanistan (FW), Colombia (FW), Lebanon (FW), Tajikistan (FW)

United Nations Educational, Scientific and Cultural Organization (UNESCO) Afghanistan (FW)

United Nations Environment Program (UNEP) Afghanistan (FW)

United Nations High Commissioner for Refugees (UNHCR) Jordan (FW)

United Nations Human Settlements Programme (UN-Habitat) Afghanistan (LE, FW)

United Nations International Strategy for Disaster Reduction (UNISDR) Tajikistan (FW)

United Nations Office for the Coordination of Humanitarian Affairs (UN-OCHA) Afghanistan (FW)

Universidad Nacional de Colombia Colombia (FW)

Université Cheikh Anta Diop - Human Rights Institute (IDHP/UCAD) Senegal (FW)

University of the Philippines (College of Social Sciences and Philosophy) Philippines (FW)

US Agency for International Development (USAID) Lebanon (FW), Philippines (FW), USA (FW)

Vétérinaires sans Frontières Germany (VSF Germany) Kenya (LE)

Women in Law and Development Africa (WiLDAF) Mali (LE)

Working Group on Peace and Development (FriEnt) Germany (FW)

World Concern Thailand (LE)

World Food Program (WFP) Timor-Leste (FW)

World Health Organization (WHO) Kenya (LE)

World Vision Australia (FW), Bolivia (LE), Lebanon (FW), Mindanao, Philippines (LE), Philippines (FW), Sri Lanka (LE), USA (FW, C)

Youth Development Initiative Network Myanmar/Burma (LE)

Appendix 3

Issue Papers and Policy Briefs

Issue Papers

International Assistance as a Delivery System
(September 2008)
Available in English and French

The Cascading Effects of International Agendas and Priorities
(September 2008)
Available in English, French and Spanish

Presence: "Why Being Here Matters"
(September 2008)
Available in English and French

"Discuss Together, Decide Together, Work Together"
(September 2008)
Available in English and French

The Importance of Listening
(March 2010)
Available in English and Spanish

Structural Relationships in the Aid System
(March 2010)
Available in English and Spanish

The Role of Staffing Decisions
(June 2010)
Available in English

Dealing with Corruption
(February 2011)
Available in English

Perceptions of Aid in Places Affected by Conflict
(June 2011)
Available in English

Whose Development? Aid Recipient Perspectives on Ownership
(September 2011)
Available in English

Policy Briefs

The Listening Project and Good Humanitarian Donorship
(February 2011)

The Listening Project and Development Effectiveness
(February 2011)

The Listening Project and Aid Effectiveness: Aid Recipient Perspectives on the Paris Declaration
(June 2011)

Local Perceptions of International Engagement in Fragile States and Situations
(July 2011)

Partnering with the Private Sector
(September 2011)

How to Make Aid More Effective for People Affected by Conflict and Fragility
(December 2011)

Index

favoritism, 85, 86, 90, 99, 100–102, 106, 111
  government distribution of aid and, 85, 86–88, 90
  implications for aid providers, 110–13
  middlemen as consumers and conduits of aid, 44, 45, 85, 91, 92, 99–103
  nepotism, 99, 100–102, 106–7
  opportunities for, 40
  patronage, 99, 100–102, 106
  prevention of, 110
  recommendations to solve problems associated with, 111, 112
  theft and diversion, 100
  waste and misuse of resources and funds, 2, 100, 108–11, 141

D

Dakar, Senegal, feedback workshop, 150
delivery processes and systems
  attitudes and actions of recipients and, 42–44
  changes to, 2
  changes to, difficulty of, 145–46
  changes to, responsibilities for, 143–45
  duplication and redundancy, 46
  efficiency and effectiveness of, i, 1, 2, 44–45, 48
  focus on delivery and design and priorities of programs, 37–42, 44, 48–50, 52–53, 63
  focus on delivery and effects on people involved in assistance efforts, 42–45, 48–50, 110–12
  focus on delivery and purpose of aid, 46–48
  local partners and middlemen, 44, 45, 83–84, 89–98, 99–103
  objects, aid processes and treatment of recipients as, 22–23, 135–36
  opinions of recipients about, 135–36
  origins and history of, 33–34
  paradigm shift and collaborative aid system, 136–146
  prevention focus of aid and, 34–35
  speed and timeliness of aid delivery, 40, 41, 73, 107, 109–10, 111
  spending money as focus of programs, 41–42, 43, 49
  staffing of aid agencies, 144–45
  theory of change, 37, 48, 138–39

Denmark
  Copenhagen feedback workshop, 150
engagement and participation obstacles, 127
design and priorities of programs
  collaborative aid system, 137–146
  donor agendas and policies and, 51–62, 64
  fads, trends, and shifting priorities, 59–62
  focus on aid delivery and, 37–42, 44, 48–50, 52–53, 63, 92, 93
  media influence on priorities of programs, 57
  participation, ownership, and sustainability principles, 66, 67–74, 96–97
  policy-program gap, 63
  pre-packaged and template projects, 44, 70, 71, 78, 84, 133, 136, 137–38
Dili, Timor-Leste, feedback workshop, 150
donors, 4. *See also* providers (donors) of aid and international assistance
Dushanbe, Tajikistan, feedback workshop, 150

E

Ecuador
  allocation of funds and who gets aid, 118
  attitudes and actions of aid recipients, 43
  business of aid, 35, 36, 47
  collaboration of providers, 46
  communication and information sharing concerns, 116, 118, 119
  corruption and diversion issues, 106
  disincentives to move out of aid categories, 77
  donor agendas and policies and aid to, 58, 59, 60, 62
  feelings about and impacts of aid, 23, 27, 30, 31
  goals and timeframes of projects, 116
  government distribution of aid, 87
  impacts of aid, monitoring and evaluation of, 106
  listening exercise and report, 149
  local partners and middlemen and delivery of aid, 93, 94

Melbourne, Australia, feedback workshop, 150

middlemen as consumers and conduits of aid, 44, 45, 85, 91, 92, 99–103

Myanmar (Burma). *See also* Thai-Burma border
business of aid, 35
communication and information sharing concerns, 120, 122
competition among providers, 46
corruption and diversion issues, 101
design and priorities of programs, 39
donor agendas and policies and aid to, 54, 56
engagement and participation obstacles, 126
feelings about and impacts of aid, 19, 24
government distribution of aid, 88, 97
listening exercise and report, 149
participation, ownership, and sustainability of aid, 69, 70
procedure standardization and requirements, 81
speed and timeliness of aid delivery, 81

N

nepotism, 99, 100–102, 106–7
New Deal for Engagement in Fragile States, i

O

ownership, participation, and sustainability principles, 66, 67–74, 96–97

P

paradigm shift and collaborative aid system, 136–146
Paris Declaration on Aid Effectiveness, 66, 88
participation. *See* engagement and participation
partnerships and relationships
with civil society groups, 89–98
engagement obstacles, 125–133
with governments of recipients, 84–89, 96–98
healthy partnerships, 98
improvements in, 96–97, 98
limitations and negative effects of, 84, 98

local partners and middlemen and delivery of aid, 44, 45, 83–84, 89–98
presence, 49–50, 111–12, 127–28, 132
providers and recipients, relationship between, 38, 48–50, 67, 84, 111–12, 125–133, 135–36
trust, control, and, 97, 121–22

patronage, 99, 100–102, 106

Philippines
communication and information sharing concerns, 116
corruption and diversion issues, 100, 102, 109
donor agendas and policies and aid to, 57, 61
engagement and participation obstacles, 127
engagement obstacles, 125
feelings about and impacts of aid, 20, 24, 27
goals and timeframes of projects, 116
government distribution of aid, 89
impacts of aid, monitoring and evaluation of, 41, 42
Manila feedback workshop, 150
Mindanao listening exercise and report, 149
reactions to and opinions about Listening Project, 15, 16

policies. *See* agendas and policies

Policy Briefs, 160

political conditions
conflicts, jealousies, and tensions created by aid, 24–26, 31
donor policies and political isolation, 54–55, 56, 64
government distribution of aid and political power, 86–88, 101, 102
improvements in, 18–19

presence, 49–50, 111–12, 127–28, 132

procedures and proceduralization
accountability and mutual accountability principle, 65–66, 78–81
adaptation and flexibility/inflexibility of, 66, 67, 70, 72
assessment procedures, 70–71, 75–76
benefit and importance of, 65–66, 82
changes to, difficulty of, 145–46
changes to, responsibilities for, 143–45
community consultation, 71–73, 77–78
compliance with, 66–67, 82

5236497R00103

Printed in Great Britain
by Amazon.co.uk, Ltd.,
Marston Gate.